Circuit Training

are to be returned on or
the last date below.

Ulli Heldt

TIPS FOR SUCCESS
CIRCUIT TRAINING

Meyer & Meyer Sport

Original title: Tipps für Zirkeltraining
4. überarbeitete Auflage
– Aachen: Meyer und Meyer Verlag, 2001
Translated by Anne Lammert

British Library Cataloguing in Publication Data
A catalogue for this book is available from the British Library

Heldt, Ulli:
Tips for Success-Circuit Training/Ulli Heldt
[Transl.: Anne Lammert].
– Oxford : Meyer & Meyer Sport (UK) Ltd., 2001
ISBN 1-84126-028-2

© 2001 by Meyer & Meyer Sport (UK) Ltd.
Oxford, Aachen, Olten (CH), Vienna, Québec,
Lansing/Michigan, Adelaide, Auckland, Johannesburg, Budapest
Member of the World
Sportpublishers' Association

Cover Photo: Foto-Atelier Braune, Bad Segeberg
Illustrations: Ulli Heldt
Cover design: Birgit Engelen, Stolberg
Cover and type exposure: frw, Reiner Wahlen, Aachen
Editorial: Winfried Vonstein
Printed and bound in Germany
by Burgverlag Gastinger GmbH, Stolberg
ISBN 1-84126-028-2
e-mail: verlag@meyer-meyer-sports.com

Contents

1 Many Thanks

To all the trainers and sports instructors who gave me such positive feedback on the previous editions of this book, I would like to say a big thank you. This great enthusiasm has encouraged me to include new trends in this new extended and revised edition. New exercises and two more sample lessons are intended to extend the trainer's range of exercises as well as bringing him more up to date.

A huge thank you goes out to my friends and colleagues from Teamwork. I would particularly like to thank Lexie Griffiths, Esben Aalvik, Daniel Koch and Marco Weiß for their exceptional support, thorough feedback and for the wonderful enthusiasm. Their energy and creativity is really contagious.

2 Circuit Training – Drill or Effective Training?

Who is not familiar with the following scene at school? "Circuit training is on the agenda today. You can start setting up the equipment!" A sense of dismay fills the room. Previously beaming faces suddenly drop as all enthusiasm for the sports lesson diminishes. Everyone knows: today I'm going to have my utmost squeezed out of me – and tomorrow I'll be so stiff that I won't be able to move with the pain.

How lucky we are that there are other methods available!
Giving the right dose of circuit training it can even be fun. And that's true, not only for all age groups but for all training conditions (or lack of them): the important thing is that the participants are made aware of the following: they should each train within their own load range. Basically this means doing the exercises and still having fun, as well as being able to have a little chat if necessary (see chapter "The theoretical background"). This fact gives us a simple but effective concept for carrying out circuit training. A structure is chosen which allows for alternatives for both beginners and advanced participants. As long as the different load intensities of the main forms of physical demand e.g. general endurance, maximal strength, flexibility, are considered when selecting exercises, everyone can have a good time.

2.1 About the Contents of this Book

This book is designed to offer theoretical and practical help for the planning and carrying-out of a circuit training lesson. The basic requirements as regards the external factors e.g room capacity and equipment, are dealt with first, as well as internal factors such as the participants' target group and the trainer's own personality.

The second half contains the exercise sheets which describes the exercises on two pages. The diagrams have been deliberately kept simple, thus easy to follow. When drawn out and enlarged they can be used as a guideline for the participants at each station.

As well as a description of the exercises, the errors which may occur, and possible variations for beginners and advanced participants, there is also an apparatus arrangement for the individual exercises catering for one person per phase. However alternatives to this are offered in some cases. Assessing the proportion of the main motor demands on one's physical load plays a further important role. Whichever training goal is being pursued with the circuit, be it endurance or maximal strength for example, can be taken from this table. It must be mentioned here however that load perception can be quite different and subjective. The table nevertheless gives the trainer an idea.

The third part contains descriptions of prepared and tested lessons.They are in random order, but designed for different target groups and training goals. In addition to a short description with relevant comments there are also suggestions as to the order of events and the organisation. A listing of all necessary equipment including sketches provides an overall view of how to plan circuit training in a simplified way.

3 Essential Requirements before Carrying out Circuit Training

3.1 Theoretical Background

Assuming that **medium-load intensities** and **numerous variations** in the exercises are the most effective form of training for fitness and health, training within a circle is then exactly the right choice. There are endless opportunities for variable training arrangements. By altering individual exercises or the entire structure, or by way of different time intervals, the main focus of the training goal (e.g. endurance, strength endurance, flexibility or even coordination) can also be easily altered.

With so many possibilities of varying the load it is difficult to categorise circuit training within a programme covering all forms of training. Deciding between extensive or intensive interval training, general endurance, strength endurance or maximal strength training, depends on the above-mentioned factors. Several examples of this can be found among the lessons suggested in the fourth part of this book.

The load for health-orientated fitness training (special training for competitive sport is not taken into account here) lies within a range of 60-85% maximal heart rate or maximal strength. Variations within this range can be made depending on performance ability and physical condition. In order to avoid an overload, a beginner for example should train at between 60-70% of his maximal performance ability, whereas an advanced participant may train at up to 85%.

Recommended are pulse watches from the company Polar with Own Zone function. These measure heart rate and automatically calculate the effective and safe level of intensity for training. The individual setting is based on the variation in heart rate, a new scientifically safeguarded process for determining the current optimal training ability.

Aside from all the calculations and confusing formulas for finding the right frequency of training or strength loads, it is important not to forget that the personal, **subjective perception of exertion** is an important, if not the most important, guide towards suitable training intensity.

3.2 The Load Intervals

Assuming medium-load intensities in each case, the following intervals would be suitable for the average participant:

> 60 seconds load
> 20 seconds rest (or move to the next station)

These time intervals must be adapted naturally according to both the relevant target group and training goal:

Sport beginners and older participants:	30 - 40 sec. load	30 sec. rest
Children:	40 - 60 sec. load	20 sec. rest
Maximal strength training:	20 - 30 sec. load	30 sec. rest
Endurance training:	60 - 120 sec. load	15 sec. rest

3.3 Structure of the Lesson

For a better understanding, here is a description of the course of events in a *typical* circuit training lesson (60 min):

5 min   *Setting up plus a few words of explanation*
In order to have more time for the training itself, it's better to have the circuit already set up before the lesson. If this is not possible then all participants should help out, the trainer keeping an overall view. An explanation of the exercises at the beginning of the lesson is preferable to one after the warm-up, as this could result in cooling.

10 min   *Warm-up*
This is to prepare the body physically and mentally for the oncoming physical effort. Exercises from the circuit (or simulation of them) can be introduced here e.g. step combinations from aerobics, semi-squats, press-ups (simulated standing upright), biceps curls, lunge steps, step-aerobics steps etc.

11 min   *Station training*
During this part of the lesson participants train in twos and threes at a particular station. After each load interval the

participants move on in a clockwise direction to the next station. Run of events: e.g. for 8 stations: 8 x 1min. load plus 8 x 20 sec rest (or move to the next station).

8 min Group training

After participants have been at all stations once, a good thing to have now is an "active break" whereby all the participants, now all facing the front, are trained together.

For example:

a) general endurance training, e.g. aerobics choreography, walking, rope skipping

b) strength endurance exercises e.g. training of abdominal, back, leg muscles or similar

11 min Station training

This phase can ideally be varied as follows:

a) to be carried out exactly as the first station training

b) to be carried out at a higher degree of difficulty and/or longer load duration.

5 min Cool down

This part of the lesson serves to either slowly reduce the heart rate or to gradually ease off in general e.g. through loosening-up exercises or walking movements.

10 min Stretching

Particularly those groups of muscles which were mainly worked on in the circuit training should be stretched here.

In order to keep motivation levels up, two rounds of the circuit are normally enough. A further round, although for advanced participants vey effective, is not in line with the fun aspect of the whole thing and could be just too much for beginners. The decision to carry out group training between or after a session of station training can be made according to the time and the trainer's and participants' preferences. It may also be left out completely. More details of or deviations from this basic concept can be found in Chapter 5 "Sample lessons".

▨▨▨▨▨ 3.4 The Trainer[1]

Obviously it is understood that the trainer is expected to know the basic steps of a sports lesson. Knowledge in the areas of sports medicine and training theory, but also of method and teaching skills are, along with other factors, important.

Apart from these important "technical" prerequisites, the trainer's personality and aura are also of great significance for the success of the lesson. What makes a trainer stand out is his/her ability to motivate without overtaxing, to spur on without ordering about, and to be funny and witty without appearing to be hyped up. **Be a leader pushing and encouraging, and not a speaking clock!**

▨▨▨▨▨ 3.5 The Participants

One could write novels about the groups of participants – but preferably not. How to handle a group, be it from a methodical, didactic, educational or other point of view, is a decision which the trainer will make individually anyway. One always hopes however that they will all appear again for the next lesson!

The lessons described at the end of this book cater mostly for 18 participants. If more arrive than initially expected the number of stations or the number of persons at each station is increased. A group which is mixed i.e. with beginners and advanced, will involve slightly more work for the trainer. He must draw on the many alternatives and variations possible and find suitable exercises for the individual participants but still not lose his general overview. A share of tact, empathy and experience are necessary here in order to be able to push and demand but also to put on the brakes at an optimal level when necessary.

However circuit training is a form of sports where it is relatively easy to give one's time and attention to the participants. For example the stations may be set up with steps at different heights or with different exertubes so that everyone can train within their optimal range.

---

1 To avoid misunderstanding: the term "trainer" applies to trainers, training supervisors, teachers and all other sports instructors, male and female.

A particularly optimal way of varying the lessons is through the use of flexible, wobbly „cushions" for sitting on, lying on or standing on. They can, for example, be used instead of steps or directly on the steps. They are just as good for stomach exercises, for press-ups or coordination exercises.

Including these flexible cushions in a lesson represents a new challenge and raises the stimulative nature of it all. Furthermore the many different positive effects are a better sense of balance, quicker muscle build-up, steadier joints, improved posture and coordination. As the quality of these cushions should be high, use of the multi-functional Aero-Steps from B.CO. They are approximately 60 cm x 40 cm in size, consist of two separate air pockets with round „nubbles" to improve blood circulation.

3.6 The Room and the Equipment

The exercises suggested have been deliberately designed to be carried out both in a sports hall and a fitness studio. Relatively little space is required; 150 m^2 - 200 m^2 for 20 participants would be sufficient. Most of the pieces of apparatus chosen are part of the normal fitness studio equipment and there are generally plenty of them available. If they are not all available one can use a bit of imagination and invent equally good alternatives. To keep up the stimulative nature of circuit training certain "alternative" pieces of apparatus are particularly suitable, such as juggling cloths, frisbees, balloons or beanbags. Here is a summary and a brief description of the apparatus necessary:

Exertubes (1) = stretchable rubber tubes with firm handles.
Each colour symbolizes a different strength: yellow = easy, green = medium, red = difficult, blue = very difficult. The green exertubes are suitable for the majority of the exercises. Physio-bands (normally used in physiotherapy) provide a useful alternative to exertubes as may a magician's cord.

Rubber bands (2) = simple rubber bands with different strengths (some people maintain that they look like big blue rubber rings used for sealing jars) or of towelled elastic. Again one could alternatively use physio-bands or Deuser bands. The exerings (Xerings) available in sports shops, rings made of exertube material with foam handles, are also very suitable.

Steps (3) = a step or platform with an adjustable height. The Reebok step as an example can be distinguished from others due to its good non-slip surface and durable material. When there are no steps available, box-tops can be used (be careful, they are higher and wider!).

Beanbags = little cotton bags filled with beans, peas, cherry stones, rice or similar. Hint: peas are cheaper than beans! Enjoy the needlework!

Dumb-bells (4) = small handweights from 400 g to 5 kg, mainly vinyl-coated. Plastic bottles filled with sand or water are an alternative.

Balloons (5) can be found in every toy shop, and even perhaps the clasps so that they can be used again. You could also maybe ask for a sponsor!?

Sticks (6) = professional gymnastic sticks made of wood or plastic, or broomsticks. Sometimes a hand towel, rolled up and tautly held, can also be used.

Skipping Ropes (7) = plastic ropes for fast skips with little strength effort. The classic skipping ropes from the sports halls can of course also be used.

Small balls (8) = tennis balls or any plastic balls of a similar size can be used in a variety of ways.

Juggling cloths (9) = very light nylon cloths approx. 50 cm x 50 cm. Alternative: why not give Granny's hair net a go?!

Pezzi balls (10) = balls to sit on, of firm material. Also known as fit-balls or physio-balls.

Water-balls (11) = beach-balls, slow motion balls for playing and rollicking about.

Mats (12) = The most suitable here are light isomats or professional gymnastic mats which are durable but still light.

Rebounders = small round trampolines with a firm jumping mat with securely covered steel springs.

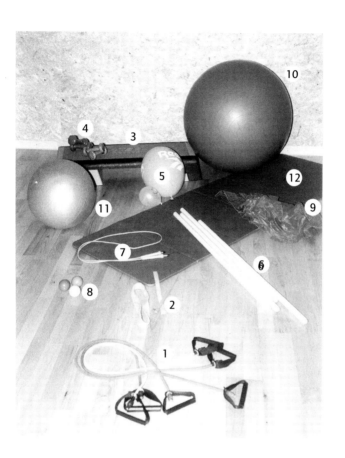

Long dumb-bells = 140 cm long light rods with adjustable weight discs, which are easy to change and can vary from 1.25 kg to 5 kg pro disc.

Slides = sliding mats on which one can slide to and fro with the use of special socks worn over the shoes. As an alternative one can use carpet tiles or juggling cloths.

Aero-Steps = flexible air cushions for training balance and neuromuscular co-ordination. These wobbly bases are about 60 x 40 cm in size, 10 cm high and consist of two separate air pockets.
Frisbees, badminton games, beachball games, softballs not to mention slides and numerous other pieces of apparatus give an idea of the almost unendless array of possibilities one has in circuit training. Besides, the great advantage of circuit training is the fact that one doesn't need to have 20 different pieces of apparatus available but rather 2-4 per station instead.

3.7 Music

There is no doubt that circuit training is much better with music. The question arises however as to finding the right music style. Good luck here! Special circuit training CDs are particularly suitable as they are put together to fit in with the load intervals. The trainer thus avoids having to constantly look at his watch and is able to devote all his time to the participants. Recommended speeds lie between 120 and 130 bpm.

2 bpm refers to beats (of music) per minute.

4 Suggested Exercises

Some of the most common and suitable exercises for circuit training are listed on the following pages. Obviously this list of exercises is by no means complete, but it does provide a general overview and is thus a help when planning a lesson. For extending your collection of exercises please use the sheet at the end of this chapter which can in turn be copied and filled with ideas of your own.

Here is a summary of the suggested exercises with page number, together with rough indications of the main muscle groups being worked on in each case.

Focus on Trunk Muscles		Page
Sit-ups	Upright abdominal muscles	22
Sit-ups	Oblique abdominal muscles	24
Foot Slides	Upright abdominal muscles	26
Hip Lifts	Entire abdominal muscles	28
Sit-ups (in twos)	Upright abdominal muscles	30
Hip Side Lifts	Lateral trunk muscles	32
Horizontal Lever	Entire trunk muscles	34
Back Lifts	Upright back muscles	36
Arm Side Lifts	Upper back muscles	38
Rowing	Upper back muscles	40
Stick Pulling	Upper back muscles	42
Rubber Band Pulling	Upper back muscles	44
Do It Together	Upper back muscles	46
Focus on Shoulder, Arm and Pectoral Muscles		
Bench Presses	Pectorals	48
Flying Dumb-bells	Pectorals	50
Press-ups	Pectorals	52
Flying	Middle shoulder muscles	54
Arm Lifts (front)	Front shoulder muscles	56
Weight Lifting	Entire shoulder and neck muscles	58
Shoulder Press	Shoulder muscles	60
Arm Lifts (rear)	Rear shoulder muscles	62
Upright Rows	Entire shoulder muscles	64
Biceps Curls	Frontal humeral muscles	66
Dips	Outer humeral muscles	68
French Press	Humeral muscles	70

1 Sit-ups

M. rectus abdominus
Come up straight, leaving lower back on the floor

Apparatus
- A mat

Description of exercise
Starting position: supine position
The hands are behind the head (to give the head light support) or alongside the body, the feet are pressed firmly on the floor with the heels for a stable position.

Procedure:
Raise the upper part of the upper body i.e. head and shoulder blades (if possible) and lower again. The lower back remains on the floor. As a guideline, your eyes are directed diagonally past the knees toward the ceiling (not straight upwards).

Possible errors
- Hands pull the head up rather than supporting it.
- The neck is overstretched.
- Exercise carried out too quickly.
- The lower back loses contact with the floor.

Correction of errors
- The hands may only hold the head. Try working less forcefully with the arms.
- Eyes are focussed diagonally upwards in front of you.
- Movements to be made more slowly.
- Lay a small towel or cushion underneath the lower back.

Possible variations
For beginners:
- Hands push forward over the knees (easier to manage but hard on the neck muscles)

For advanced:
- Arms are held stretched out either behind or beside the head.

Proportion of main motor forms of demand on physical load			
	low	medium	high
gen. endurance:	x		
strength endurance:			x
maximal strength:		x	
speed:	x		
flexibility:	x		
co-ordination:	x		

Hint
Good preparation for a skiing holiday!

!

2 Sit-ups

M.obliquus externitus abdominis, M.obliquus internus abdominis
Come up to the left and right, lower back remains on the floor

Apparatus
- A mat

Description of exercise
Starting position: supine position
The right hand is behind the head to give light support to the neck, the left arm stretched out across the floor. The right foot is pressed firmly on the floor with the heel to aid stabilization, the left ankle rests on the right knee.

Procedure:
Raise and lower head and right shoulder blade. The movement is in a diagonal direction all the time, i.e. the right shoulder moves towards the left knee. The lower back stays on the floor throughout the exercise. As a guideline eyes are directed past the outer side of the right thigh. The exercise should be carried out with the same number of times on both sides.

Possible errors
- Hands pull at the head.
- The neck is overstretched.
- Exercise is carried out too quickly.
- The lower back loses contact with the floor.
- Sidewards turning instead of a diagonal movement.

Correction of errors

- The hands may only hold the head. Work less forcefully with the arms.
- The eyes are directed diagonally upwards.
- Movements are conducted more slowly.
- Lay a small towel or cushion underneath the lower back.
- The movement is more to the knee than to the side.

Possible variations

For beginners:

- Hands push forward past the thigh (easier to manage but very straining on the neck and cervical muscles).

For advanced:

- Arms are held stretched behind or beside the head.
- The legs are held upright.

Proportion of main motor forms of demand on physical load			
	low	medium	high
gen. endurance:	x		
strength endurance:			x
maximal strength:		x	
speed:	x		
flexibility:		x	
co-ordination:		x	

Hint

Repeating the exercise a number of times on each side prevents dizziness!

!

3 Foot Slides

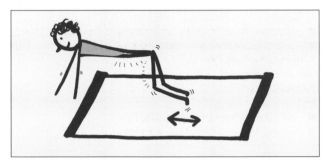

M. rectus abdominus
Slowly and steadily crouch the knees in!

Apparatus
- Two carpet tiles/ juggling cloths/ paper towels or a slide.

Description of exercise
Starting position: press-up position
The hands are placed on the floor at shoulder width, the arms are lightly bent. The head is an extension of the spinal column at all times. The feet are on a slippery surface such as juggling cloths or a slide. The knees are raised and are approximately 1cm away from the floor.

Procedure:
Without any sweeping movement the knees are crouched in towards the body and then stretched back out again. The movement is achieved through the strength of the abdominal muscles.

Possible errors
- The legs are crouched in with a sweeping movment.
- The elbows are stretched.
- The head is hanging down.
- When the legs are stretched out , the upper body sags.
- The knees are too far away from the floor.

Correction of errors

- Slow, powerful crouching of the legs.
- The arms are slightly bent.
- The head stays in line with the spine. Eyes are directed toward the floor.
- Shoulders and posterior remain horizontal, the stomach is tensed.
- Keep up more tension in the abdominal muscles. The knees are grazing the floor surface.

Possible variations

For beginners:

- The knees are further away from the floor.
- The legs are not stretched out completely.

For advanced:

- Stretch the legs out behind and follow the movement up with a press-up.
- Very advanced participants can do this exercise on one leg.

Proportion of main motor forms of demand on physical load			
	low	medium	high
gen. endurance:	X		
strength endurance:		X	
maximal strength:			X
speed:	X		
flexibility:		X	
co-ordination:		X	

Hint

A very intensive exercise – tensing of a lot of muscles is necessary.

!

4 Hip Lifts

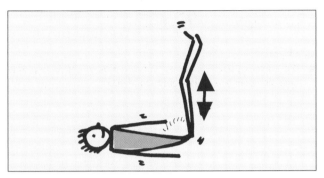

M.rectus abdominus
Raise hips, stretching feet up towards the ceiling

Apparatus
- A mat

Description of exercise
Starting position: supine position
Hands are at the neck or alongside the body. Legs are (almost)
stretched out towards the ceiling.

Procedure:
Raise and lower pelvis gently from the floor. The heels are stretched
upwards at all times, the upper body remains on the floor. The
movement is correctly done by tightening the abdominals and is not a
sweeping movement.

Possible errors
- Sweeping movements.
- Legs are pulled towards the body.

Correction of errors
- The exercise is to be carried out more slowly and accurately.
- The soles of the feet are directed towards the ceiling during the
  exercise.

Possible variations

For beginners:

- Tightening and relaxing of the abdominals only.
- Drawing the legs slowly towards the body. The above variation is carried out in the supine position on a sloped step, whereby the upper body is lower than the pelvis.

For advanced:

- The above variation is carried out again on a sloped step; this time the upper body is higher than the pelvis.

Proportion of main motor forms of demand on physical load			
	low	medium	high
gen. endurance:	x		
strength endurance:		x	
maximal strength:			x
speed:	x		
flexibility:			x
co-ordination:			x

Hint

A difficult and exerting (sometimes frustrating) exercise – more of an exercise for the advanced!

!

5 Sit-ups (in twos)

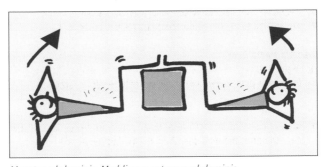

M.rectus abdominis, M.obliquus externus abdominis,
M.obliquus internus abdominis
Come up straight or diagonally, heels are pressed onto the step

Apparatus
- A high step/small box/bench
- Two mats

Description of exercise
Starting position: supine position
The hands are behind the head (to give the head light support) or alongside the body, the feet are pressed firmly on the step with the heels for a stable position.

Procedure:
Raise and lower upper part of upper body i.e. head and shoulder blades (when possible). The lower back remains on the floor throughout the exercise. As a guide, eyes are directed diagonally past the knees towards the ceiling and not straight up.

Possible errors
- The hands pull the head instead of supporting it.
- The neck is overstretched.
- The movements are carried out too quickly.
- The lower back loses contact with the floor.

Correction of errors:

- The hands may only hold the head. Try working less forcefully with the arms.
- The eyes are to be directed diagonally upwards in front of you.
- The movements are to be conducted more slowly.
- Lay a small towel or cushion underneath the lower back.

Possible variations

For beginners:

- The hands pull up over the knees or try to reach the step.

For advanced:

- The exercise is done with additional strong foot pressure on the step. The arms are held stretched out behind the head.

Proportion of main motor forms of demand on physical load			
	low	medium	high
gen. endurance:	x		
strength endurance:			x
maximal strength:		x	
speed:	x		
flexibility:		x	
co-ordination:		x	

Hint

Training in twos (or threes) on the one piece of apparatus is a lot more fun – good for beginners!

!

6 Hip Side Lifts

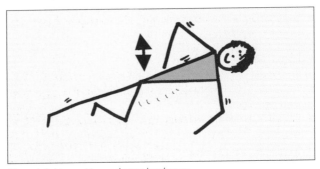

Mm. abduktores, M. quadratus lumborum,
M. abdominis,: erector spinae
Lateral position only

Apparatus
- A mat

Description of exercise
Starting position: lateral position with forearm support
The right elbow is vertically under the right shoulder. For a more stable position the right leg is bent, the left leg is stretched and touching the floor with the toes.
The shoulder muscles are tensed and the spine is straight to avoid the back sagging.

Procedure:
Raise the pelvis from the floor and move up and down. One must pay attention not to let the upper body fall forwards. So: the left leg and the upper body form a straight line. The cervical spine and head continue this line. After a while change sides.

Possible errors
- Tilting forwards or backwards.
- Sinking into the shoulders.
- Difficulties visualizing the correct movement.

Correction of errors

- Upper body and leg are one line.
- Push the shoulders down while stretching the neck at the same time.
- Give a visual interpretation of the exercise. e.g. a string at the hip pulls the upper body upwards. Only the forearm and lower leg have floor contact.

Possible variations

For beginners:

- The exercise can be made easier when the arm on top is placed in front for support.
- Instead of movement, the tensed position can also be held.

For advanced:

- Raise the leg on top.
- Stretch the leg underneath so that one can only prop oneself up on the foot.

Proportion of main motor forms of demand on physical load			
	low	medium	high
gen. endurance:	x		
strength endurance:		x	
maximal strength:		x	
speed:	x		
flexibility:	x		
co-ordination:			x

Hint
Overweight people don't like this exercise much!

!

7 Horizontal Lever

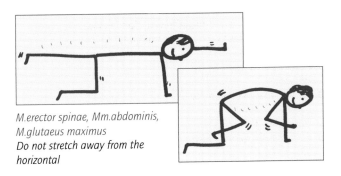

M.erector spinae, Mm.abdominis, M.glutaeus maximus
Do not stretch away from the horizontal

Apparatus
- A mat

Description of exercise
Starting position: quadruped stand
The right arm is stretched out in front, the left leg to the back. Toes are pointing downwards. The head and the cervical spine are a continuation of the spinal column. The supporting left arm is lightly bent. The body weight is centred and does not shift to the side.

Procedure:
The right arm and the left leg are simultaneously drawn towards the body.
The back becomes round. When spreading arm and leg out the back is stretched again.
After a while change sides.

Possible errors
- The right arm and the right leg are raised.
- A hollow back can be the result of exaggerated stretching of arm and leg.
- Loss of balance.
- The neck is overstretched.
- Quick, sweeping movement.

Correction of errors

- Emphasise the 'diagonal' feature of the exercise.
- The arm, upper body and the raised leg form a straight line.
- Stress that the stretched position is held by tensing the trunk muscles.
- The head is also in line with the raised arm and leg.
- The movements are conducted more slowly.

Possible variations

For beginners:

- Move either one arm or leg.

For advanced:

- Carry out the exercise with hand, and anklecuffs.

Proportion of main motor forms of demand on physical load			
	low	medium	high
gen. endurance:	x		
strength endurance:			x
maximal strength:		x	
speed:	x		
flexibility:		x	
co-ordination:			x

Hint

A popular exercise for spine gymnastics

!

8 Back Lifts

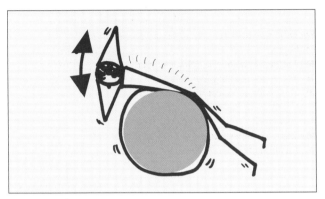

M. erector spinae
Do not overstretch the spinal column, keep abdominal muscles slightly tensed

Apparatus
- A pezziball, 65 cm

Description of exercise
Starting position: prone position on the ball
The upper body must 'hang down' over the ball. The legs are slightly straddled and the feet remain on the floor to keep the position stable. The hands are held at the neck.

Procedure:
Roll up from the rounded position of the spinal column to a stretched one and roll down again. The feet and the ball remain in the same position at all times.

Possible errors
- The entire spinal column is overstretched.
- The cervical spine is also overstretched, the head is held up too far.
- The starting position is too high.

Correction of errors
- Only raise the back as much as is necessary i.e. so that the thighs and the back form a straight line.
- Eyes are directed towards the floor.
- The toes should only just be able to reach the floor.

Possible variations
For beginners:
- The hands are on the ball for support.
- The arms are alongside the body.
- The hands are under the forehead.

For advanced:
- The hands are stretched out in front.
- Addition of (light) dumb-bells.

Proportion of main motor forms of demand on physical load			
	low	medium	high
gen. endurance:	x		
strength endurance:			x
maximal strength:		x	
speed:	x		
flexibility:			x
co-ordination:		x	

Hint
Don't eat so much beforehand!

!

9 Arm Side Lifts

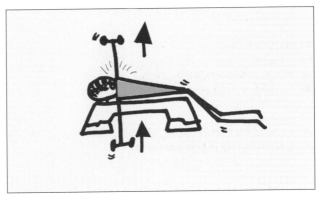

M.trapezius, Mm. rhomboideus
Upper body stays on the step, head is an extension of the spine

Apparatus
- A high step/bench/box top with one inlay
- A mat
- Two light dumb-bells

Description of exercise
Starting position: prone position on step
The knees are on the ground, the head is kept in line with the spine, the arms are out to the side. The back is kept stable by tensing both abdominal and posterior muscles.

Procedure:
Raise and lower arms. The upper body remains on the step at all times.

Possible errors
- The arms are pushed back diagonally.
- The head and neck are hunched up.
- Unsuitable weights (i.e. too heavy) are being used.
- The upper body is also raised.

Correction of errors
- The upper body and arms form a 90° angle.
- Eyes are directed to the floor.
- Choose weights which one can lift at least 20 times.
- The breastbone does not lose contact with the step. Abdominal muscles are tensed.

Possible variations
For beginners:
- Exercise is done without the weights.
- The arms are close to the body and pull upwards.

For advanced:
- As an addition the shoulderblades are pulled together.The arms are stretched out in front and raised.

Proportion of main motor forms of demand on physical load			
	low	medium	high
gen. endurance:	X		
strength endurance:		X	
maximal strength:			X
speed:	X		
flexibility:		X	
co-ordination:		X	

Hint
An unpopular exercise - but effective!

!

10 Rowing

M. trapezius, Mm. rhomboideus,
M. biceps brachii, M. erector spinae
Back straight, pull back the elbows

Apparatus
- A step/small box/bench/box top
- An exertube (green or red)

Description of exercise
Starting position: sitting position at the edge of the step
Hold the back straight and upright. The legs are slightly bent and the heels are pushed onto the floor. The exertube is tied once around each foot, the hands are holding the handles or, to intensify the exercise, the rubber tube itself.

Procedure:
The elbows pull behind and the shoulder blades are pushed together. The upper arms move back, always very close to the body.

Possible errors
- The back is held in a rounded position.
- The exertubes are not tight enough around the feet.
- The shoulders are pulled up.
- The entire back is moved forward and backward.

Correction of errors
- Lift the chest a little and press the shoulders slightly together.
- Wrap the tubes tightly around the feet.
- The very important thing in the movement is to pull back the shoulders.
- The upper body must be kept in a firm, upright position.

Possible variations
For beginners:
- Use easier (yellow) exertubes.
- Raising a step makes it easier to stay in an upright position.

For advanced:
- Use more difficult (red, blue) exertubes.
- When there are no exertubes available, two rubber bands do just as good a job.

Proportion of main motor forms of demand on physical load			
	low	medium	high
gen. endurance:	x		
strength endurance:		x	
maximal strength:			x
speed:	x		
flexibility:		x	
co-ordination:		x	

Hint
Wrapping the exertube around the feet is really important – it prevents constantly slipping off it.

11 Stick Pulling

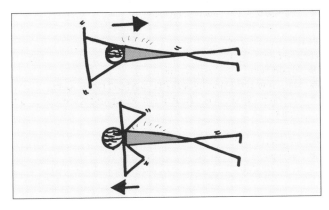

M. erector spinae, M. trapezius,
Mm. rhomboideus, M. latissimus dorsi
Stomach muscles are tensed, don't forget to breathe

Apparatus
- A gymnast's wand/stick
- A mat

Description of exercise
Starting position: prone position
The abdominal and posterior muscles are tensed so as to stabilize the spinal column.
The head is a continuation of the spine. Arms are stretched out in front of the body. The hands grip the stick at both ends.

Procedure:
Move the stick backward towards the neck and stretch again. Try not touching the floor at all. The upper body remains firmly on the floor.

Possible errors
- The upper body is raised too.
- The body is twisted sideways.
- The head is turned to the side.

Correction of errors

- The chest must be touching the floor at all times. The abdominals are tensed.
- The stick is only pulled as far as the head.
- Observe how the neck is stretched.

Possible variations

For beginners:

- Do the exercise without the stick.
- Only raise and lower the stick (the arms can remain bent).
- Lead the stick only as far as the forehead and then stretch out again.

For advanced:

- Two sticks (more weight).

Proportion of main motor forms of demand on physical load			
	low	medium	high
gen. endurance:	x		
strength endurance:		x	
maximal strength:			x
speed:	x		
flexibility:			x
co-ordination:		x	

Hint

Requires a lot of flexibility in the shoulder girdle – good for advanced participants!

!

12 Rubber Band Pulling

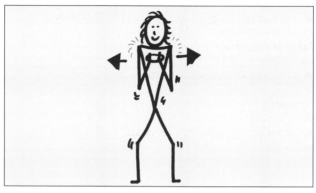

M.trapezius, Mm. rhomboideus, M. deltoideus
Back straight, legs bent, shoulders down

Apparatus
- A rubber band (narrow or wide)

Description of exercise
Starting position: upright standing position
The legs are slightly bent. The upper arms and the back are straight. The abdominal and posterior muscles are tensed to give stable position. The upper and lower arm form a right angle in front of the body.

Procedure:
Steadily and evenly extend the band and bring it together again. The important thing to watch here is that the band is not held loosely at any time, there is always tension on it.

Possible errors
- The shoulders are pulled up.
- Quick sweeping movements of the rubber band.
- There isn't permanent tension on the rubber band.
- The upper body leans back.

Correction of errors
- Very important in the exercise is the pulling back of the shoulder blades.
- The movements to be carried out more slowly.
- The movements are steady and even.
- Pay attention to upright posture. Keep the abdominals tensed.

Possible variations

For beginners:
- Green exertubes are less resistent.

For advanced:
- Firmer bands.
- Combine with leg exercises e.g. squats.

Proportion of main motor forms of demand on physical load			
	low	medium	high
gen. endurance:	x		
strength endurance:		x	
maximal strength:			x
speed:	x		
flexibility:	x		
co-ordination:		x	

Hint
An exercise which is easy to learn - watch for correct posture!

13 Do It Together

M. trapezius, Mm. rhomboideus, M. deltoideus
Don't pull with the entire body, straight posture

Apparatus
- Two narrow rubber bands/or exertubes

Description of exercise
Starting position: two participants stand opposite each other and hold a rubber band together in one hand.
Stride or a slight straddle position is advised. Firmly tensing the abdominal muscles keeps the back straight.

Procedure:
In a straight upright position both participants evenly pull the elbows back (as in rowing) and bring forward again, the shoulders pulled together at all times. During the exercise it is important to watch that the upper arms are close to the body while sliding back and forth.

Possible errors
- The whole body is pulling.
- The partners are not working evenly.
- The shoulders are pulled up.

Correction of errors

- Only the arms move behind. The upper body maintains its position.
- The trainer should indicate the correct rhythm of movement.
- Very important in this exercise is the pulling back of the shoulder blades.

Possible variations

For beginners:

- Green or yellow exertubes are more flexible.
- Only use one exertube/rubber band.

For advanced:

- Pull the outstretched arm behind.
- Pull the elbows or outstretched arms in other directions (e.g. upwards).

Proportion of main motor forms of demand on physical load			
	low	medium	high
gen. endurance:	X		
strength endurance:		X	
maximal strength:			X
speed:	X		
flexibility:		X	
co-ordination:			X

Hint
This won't work without a feeling for rhythm!

!

14 Bench Presses

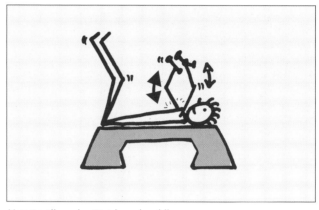

M.pectoralis major, M. triceps brachii
The entire back stays down

Apparatus
- A step/box top
- A mat
- Two dumb-bells (from 3 kg)/a medicine ball/long dumb-bell

Description of exercise
Starting position: supine position on the step
For a more comfortable position the legs are in the air. The head is lying in a relaxed position. The hands, holding two weights, are resting on the shoulders.

Procedure:
The arms raise the weights upwards until the elbows are almost fully stretched. The arms are moved evenly up and down.

Possible errors
- If feet are on the floor, the back quickly becomes hollow.
- Loss of balance.
- The arms are stretched completely.

Correction of errors

- Hold the feet up as high as is necessary to take the strain off the spine.
- Do the exercise on the floor.
- Emphasise the correct arm position.

Possible variations

For beginners:
- Light weights.
- The feet are up against the wall (supports balance).

For advanced:
- Heavier weights.

Proportion of main motor forms of demand on physical load			
	low	medium	high
gen. endurance:	x		
strength endurance:		x	
maximal strength:			x
speed:	x		
flexibility:		x	
co-ordination:			x

Hint
A classic bodybuilding exercise!

15 Flying Dumb-bells

M.pectoralis major, M. biceps brachii
Not a sweeping movement

Apparatus
- Two steps (adjustable in height)/two box tops and two box inlays
- Two dumb-bells (from 3 kg)

Description of exercise
Starting position: supine position on the step
The feet are on a higher step. The arms are almost fully stretched in a 90° angle to the side of the body. The hands are holding light weights.

Procedure:
The arms are brought together up over the body. The elbows do not meet.

Possible errors
- Quick sweeping movements.
- The elbows are bent.
- Hollow back.
- The arms are completely stretched or reach too far behind.

Correction of errors
- Concentrate on a slow movement.
- The angle between upper and lower arm is maintained.
- Pay particular attention to the back, that it stays on the step.
- A slight bend at the elbow should be kept at all times.

Possible variations
For beginners:
- Light weights.

For advanced:
- Heavy weights.

Proportion of main motor forms of demand on physical load			
	low	medium	high
gen. endurance:	x		
strength endurance:		x	
maximal strength:			x
speed:	x		
flexibility:		x	
co-ordination:		x	

Hint
Setting up is a toil!

!

16 Press-ups

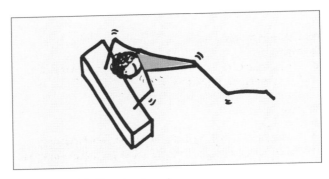

M. triceps brachii, M. pectoralis major
Tighten the stomach, no sagging

Apparatus
- A step/bench/small box
- A mat

Description of exercise
Starting position: quadruped stand
The hands rest on the step, turned in slightly. The knees are (if necessary cushioned) on a mat. The lower legs may be strongly bent at the knee to take some of the pressure off the kneecaps. The thighs and the upper body almost form a straight line. The abdominal, back and posterior muscles are tensed to prevent the body sagging down.

Procedure:
The arms are bent and then stretched. One must make sure here that the joints don't "click into place".

Possible errors
- The pelvis sags.
- The shoulders are not stable enough.
- The head hangs down.
- The arms are overstretched.

Correction of errors

- Maintain strong stomach tension.
- Tense trunk and back muscles.
- The head and the neck are a continuation of the spine.
- Stretch the arms only, don't overstretch.

Possible variations

For beginners:

- The higher the step, the easier it is to carry out the movement.
- The arms are only bent half-way.

For advanced:

- Lower step.
- The legs are stretched so that only the feet take the weight.
- The feet or the knees are placed on the step and the hands on the floor.

Proportion of main motor forms of demand on physical load			
	low	medium	high
gen. endurance:	x		
strength endurance:		x	
maximal strength:			x
speed:	x		
flexibility:		x	
co-ordination:		x	

Hint

Intensive training for the pectorals!

!

17 Flying

M. deltoideus
Work only with strength, not too high

Apparatus
■ Two dumb-bells (from 2 kg)

Description of exercise
Starting position: upright standing position
The legs are slightly straddled and slightly bent. The posterior and abdominal muscles are tensed to a degree. Arms are held down low and in each hand is a dumb-bell.

Procedure:
The arms are brought up to the shoulders and down again. There is a slight bend at the elbows and the back of the hands face upwards. An upturning of the forearms is allowed.

Possible errors
■ Quick sweeping movements.
■ The upper body begins to lean back.
■ The shoulders are pulled up.
■ The elbows are overstretched.

Correction of errors

- Slower, more accurate movements are necessary.
- Stress the tensing of the abdominal muscles in particular.
- Only the arms move upwards.
- A slight bending at the elbows should be maintained throughout.

Possible variations

For beginners:

- Use light weights.
- Raise each arm in turn.

For advanced:

- Choose heavier weights.
- The upper body tilts slightly forward (greater involvement of the back muscles).

Proportion of main motor forms of demand on physical load			
	low	medium	high
gen. endurance:	X		
strength endurance:		X	
maximal strength:			X
speed:	X		
flexibility:		X	
co-ordination:		X	

Hint

Can also be done with exertubes!

!

18 Arm Lifts (front)

M. deltoideus
The upper body is not to lean back, shoulders are down

Apparatus
- Two dumb-bells (from 1 kg)

Description of exercise
Starting position: upright standing position
The legs are lightly straddled and slightly bent. The posterior and abdominal muscles are tensed slightly. Arms are held down low and in each hand is a dumb-bell. The backs of the hands face out in front.

Procedure:
The arms (almost fully stretched) are raised simultaneously to shoulder level and lowered again.

Possible errors
- The upper body leans back.
- Quick, sweeping movements.
- The arms are dropped, instead of being lowered.

Correction of errors

- Tilt the upper body preferably forwards.
- Slower accurate movement is the more effective.
- The arms should be consciously moved up and down at the same time.

Possible variations

For beginners:

- Practise on each arm in turn.
- Choose lighter weights.

For advanced:

- Select heavier weights.

Proportion of main motor forms of demand on physical load			
	low	medium	high
gen. endurance:	x		
strength endurance:		x	
maximal strength:			x
speed:	x		
flexibility:	x		
co-ordination:		x	

Hint

Also a suitable stabilization exercise for the spinal column.

!

19 Weight Lifting

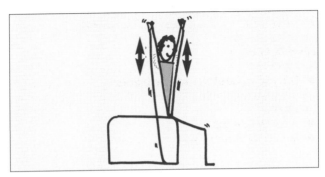

M. deltoideus, M.trapezius
The back stays straight, the shoulders stay down

Apparatus
A high step/box top and two inlays
An exertube (green)/two dumb-bells (from 3 kg)

Description of exercise
Starting position: upright sitting position on a high step
The step has the correct height when the thighs are slightly pointing downwards and the feet are firmly on the ground. The arms are in U-position i.e. the upper arms are at a 90° angle to the upper body. The lower arms are directed up (another 90° angle). The handles of the exertube are held in the hands.

Procedure:
The arms are now brought upwards without being fully stretched. When the shoulder joint is not that flexible one should try to conduct a frontal upward movement.

Possible errors
- The shoulders are pulled up.
- The arms are moved too far behind.
- The arms are brought too far down again.
- It is not possible to keep the back in a stable position.

Correction of errors

- Only the arms move upwards.
- The "frontal upward" movement can be made whereby the hands are still visible from the corner of the eye.
- The elbows may only come down to shoulder level.
- Stress in particular the tensing of the trunk muscles.

Possible variations

For beginners:

- Select lighter weights or yellow exertubes.

For advanced:

- Do the exercise standing up.
- Be careful with neck strain!

Proportion of main motor forms of demand on physical load			
	low	medium	high
gen. endurance:	x		
strength endurance:		x	
maximal strength:			x
speed:	x		
flexibility:			x
co-ordination:		x	

Hint

Be careful with neck strain!

20 Shoulder Press

M. deltoideus
Stretch the dumb-bell upward!

Apparatus
A long dumb-bell with a medium weight or a light to medium exertube.

Description of exercise
Starting position: upright standing position
The legs are lightly straddled and either slightly bent or in stride position. The dumb-bell is held in front of the chin and the hands are at shoulder width. The elbows below are straight in line with the hands.
When using an exertube, either one leg (stride position) or both legs (parallel foot position) are standing on the band. The arms are held the same way as with the dumb-bell.

Procedure:
The dumb-bell or the exertube is raised slowly and evenly. The arms are almost completely stretched, they are very slightly flexed. In the final position the dumb-bell does not end up directly over the head, but slightly in front of it. Throughout the exercise the elbows are facing forward. Ideally the elbows are at shoulder width.

Possible errors

- A hollow back.
- The arms are fully stretched.
- The elbows drift out to the side.
- The head turns to the side.
- The wrists „snap" down.

Correction of errors

- Pay attention to a good tensing of the abdominal muscles.
- In order to protect the joints the arms should be kept slightly bent.
- The elbows should be facing the front.
- Hold the head straight, reduce the weight on the dumb-bell.
- The wrists must be firm and stable. Reduce the weight on the dumb-bell.

Possible variations

For beginners:

- Use a light weight.
- The exercise is more stable if done sitting on a chair etc.

For advanced:

- Use a heavier weight.
- When lowering the dumb-bell bring it behind the head. The grasping width is then wider, the elbows are facing outwards.

Proportion of main motor forms of demand on physical load			
	low	medium	high
gen. endurance:	x		
strength endurance:		x	
maximal strength:			x
speed:	x		
flexibility:			x
co-ordination:		x	

Hint

There's no need for shoulder pads after doing this exercise!

!

21 Arm Lifts (rear)

M. deltoideus, M. trapezius, M. triceps
Maintain upright position, push the shoulders slightly forward

Apparatus
- A stick

Description of exercise
Starting position: upright standing position
The legs are lightly straddled and slightly bent. The posterior and abdominal muscles are slightly tensed. Arms are held down low, and behind the body there is a stick being held at both ends. The back of the hands are directed to the front.

Procedure:
Lift the stick back as far as possible. The arms stay stretched.

Possible errors
- In an attempt to make the exercise somewhat easier to do, the trunk is stuck out.
- The shoulders are pushed forward or pulled up.
- The wrists snap out of line.
- The whole upper body moves forward.

Correction of errors

- Preferably tilt the upper body slightly forward.
- Shoulders should be firm.
- The hands should be in line with the arms.
- The movement is performed by the arms and shoulders only.

Possible variations

For beginners:

- Pull the stick up alongside the body, bending at the elbow.

For advanced:

- Additional weightcuffs for the wrists.

Proportion of main motor forms of demand on physical load			
	low	medium	high
gen. endurance:	x		
strength endurance:		x	
maximal strength:		x	
speed:	x		
flexibility:			x
co-ordination:		x	

Hint

An exercise to get used to - but effective when carried out with strength!

!

22 Upright Rows

M. deltoideus
The shoulders stay down here too

Apparatus
- An exertube (green or red)/step/two dumb-bells (from 4 kg)

Description of exercise
Starting position: upright standing position
The legs are lightly straddled and slightly bent. The posterior and abdominal muscles are slightly tensed. Arms are held down low and hold a step or an exertube (feet stand on the exertube) and both hands grip both handles at the same time.

Procedure:
Hands pull up towards the chin. The elbows are thus pushed out to the side, the shoulders stay down.

Possible errors
- The shoulders are pulled up.
- The elbows are not moved out to the side.
- The hands are pulled up too high.
- The upper body leans back.

Correction of errors

- Only the arms move up.
- The elbows are brought to shoulder level.
- The movement is completed when the hands almost touch the chin.
- The upper body may lean forward a little.

Possible variations

For beginners:

- Use light weights.

For advanced:

- A tighter grip of the exertubes (e.g. through a wider straddle position).
- Use more difficult exertubes.

Proportion of main motor forms of demand on physical load			
	low	medium	high
gen. endurance:	x		
strength endurance:		x	
maximal strength:			x
speed:	x		
flexibility:		x	
co-ordination:		x	

Hint

Effective and not too difficult!

23 Biceps Curls

M. biceps brachii
Keep the elbows always slightly bent

Apparatus
- An exertube/two dumb-bells (from 4 kg)

Description of exercise
Starting position: upright standing position
The legs are lightly straddled and slightly bent. The posterior and abdominal muscles are slightly tensed. Arms are held down low and grasp the exertube or dumb-bell – the palms of the hands face upwards. The elbows are lightly bent.

Procedure:
Flex the forearms up to almost shoulder level (and no further). The upper arms maintain their positon.

Possible errors
- The upper body moves backwards.
- The elbows are also brought forward.
- The hands are brought up too close to the shoulders, the humeral muscles are no longer being employed.

Correction of errors

- The abdominal and back muscles are sufficiently tensed to prevent the back moving in the first place.
- The elbows are to keep their position at the waist.
- Elbows are not to be flexed too far i.e. there must be resistance.

Possible variations

For beginners:

- Use lighter weights or yellow exertubes.

For advanced:

- Upward and inward turning of the forearms.
- In the final position the upper arms are also raised to the front.

Proportion of main motor forms of demand on physical load			
	low	medium	high
gen. endurance:	x		
strength endurance:		x	
maximal strength:			x
speed:	x		
flexibility:	x		
co-ordination:		x	

Hint

Very popular exercise with men!

!

24 Dips

M. triceps brachii
Stabilize the shoulder muscles

Apparatus
■ Two steps/small boxes/benches/box tops

Description of exercise
Starting position: support position on step
The hands are behind the body on one step whereas the legs are placed on the other one. So as not to strain the wrists too much the fingers should ideally be facing to the front. The distance between the steps is such that there is a 90° angle at the hips and the knees. By tensing the abdominal, back and shoulder muscles the spinal column and the shoulder joints are stable.

Procedure:
The arms are bent and stretched at the elbow joint. The whole body moves down and up in the process.

Possible errors
■ The upper body falls down due to insufficient tensing of the shoulder muscles.
■ Only the pelvis is moved up and down.

Correction of errors

■ The neck should be pushed upwards.
■ The exercise is based on the arms being bent and stretched.

Possible variations

For beginners:

■ The feet are placed on the floor.
■ Minimal arm movements only.
■ The higher the step the hands are resting on, the easier it is to carry out the exercise.

For advanced:

■ The feet should be higher than the hands.

Proportion of main motor forms of demand on physical load			
	low	medium	high
gen. endurance:	x		
strength endurance:	x		
maximal strength:			x
speed:	x		
flexibility:			x
co-ordination:		x	

Hint

Very exerting – more suitable for the advanced class really!

25 French Press

M. triceps brachii
Stretch the arms up!

Apparatus
An exertube (green) or a rubber band.

Description of exercise
Starting position: stride position
The left foot is in front, the right foot is behind stepping on one end of the exertube. The right hand is in the handle of the exertube holding it above the head with the arm almost fully stretched.

The left hand is leaning on the left thigh for a stable position. The upper body leans slightly forward so that the right leg and the upper body form a line.

Procedure:
The almost outstretched arm is bent to form a 90° angle at the elbow. It's important to make sure that the upper arm does not lose its position beside the head and that the upper body is held in a stable and tensed position.

Possible errors
- Hollow back.
- The wrist „snaps" down.
- The elbow is bent completely.
- The upper arm sinks down.

Correction of errors
- More tensing of the abdominal muscles. Slight forward tilt of the body.
- The lower arm forms a line with the back of the hand.
- Bend only to 90°.
- The elbows should be pointing upwards.

Possible variations
For beginners:
- Use an easy exertube (yellow)

For advanced:
- Shorten the exertube so that the resistance from it is greater

Proportion of main motor forms of demand on physical load			
	low	medium	high
gen. endurance:	x		
strength endurance:		x	
maximal strength:		x	
speed:	x		
flexibility:		x	
co-ordination:			x

Hint
This strengthens not only the arms but also the trunk.

!

26 Squats

M. quadriceps, M. glutaeus maximus
Put even weight on both legs

Apparatus
■ A step/bench (for advanced)

Description of exercise
Starting position: upright standing position on a step
The feet are closed, the step is lengthways.

Procedure:
One foot takes a big step to the side.
Both legs are equally bent, the body weight is centred between the legs. The landing is soft although the hands are resting on the thighs. The heels are on the floor for a more secure position. The knees are bent in such a way that the knees point to the toes and the kneecaps are vertically above the feet, and no further.

Possible errors
■ The leg on the floor takes most of the weight.
■ The knees are turned inwards.
■ Tiptoe position because of leaning forward too much.
■ The shoulders are pulled up when the hands are on the thighs.

Correction of errors

- Equal weight to be on both legs.
- The knees are bent in the direction of the toes.
- The body weight is on the entire sole of the foot, or slightly more on the heels.
- Work less forcefully with the arms.

Possible variations

For beginners:

- Do the exercise without a step.

For advanced:

- Choose a higher step.
- Variable arm movements to include.

Proportion of main motor forms of demand on physical load			
	low	medium	high
gen. endurance:			x
strength endurance:		x	
maximal strength:		x	
speed:	x		
flexibility:	x		
co-ordination:		x	

Hint

Plyometrics exercise – very effective!

!

Frontal thigh muscles
27 Squats (in twos)

M. quadriceps, M. glutaeus maximus
Only bend to 90°

Apparatus
■ 2-3 rubber bands/one stick/hand towel

Description of exercise
Starting position: two participants stand opposite each other
They hold onto the rubber bands, towel or stick. The arms are outstretched and the body is tilted back slightly.

Procedure:
Each partner bends and stretches the legs at the same time, to a 90°angle. The movement can be compared to sitting down. The knees are not pushed forward but maintain their position.

Possible errors
■ The knees are pushed forward.
■ Reluctance to lean the body back.
■ The squats are too far down.
■ Bending and stretching rhythms differ.

74

Correction of errors

- The weight is transferred to behind.
- Practise initially with bent arms.
- The thighs no lower than the horizontal.
- Emphasise the importance of simultaneous movement.

Possible variations

For beginners:

- One partner holds the other partner (who is doing the exercise).

For advanced:

- Further bending of the arms through pulling back the elbows (only possible with stretchable material).

Proportion of main motor forms of demand on physical load			
	low	medium	high
gen. endurance:	x		
strength endurance:		x	
maximal strength:			x
speed:	x		
flexibility:	x		
co-ordination:			x

Hint
Also possible when the partners are different weights!

!

28 Mud Walking

M.quadriceps, M.glutaeus maximus
Big steps, knees always directed towards the toes

Apparatus
- None!

Description of exercise
Starting position: upright posture

Procedure:
Take big steps forward through the room. Each swinging step has a soft landing. Where necessary the hands may be placed in front on the thighs. The upper body remains upright.

Possible errors
- Small steps are taken and the squat, i.e. the bending at the knee, is too low down.
- The knees turn inwards or outwards.
- The upper body leans back.
- The legs are bent too low.

Correction of errors

- Larger steps don't strain the knee as much.
- The knees are always in line with the toes.
- Preferably lean the upper body forwards.
- The angle at the knee should be no lower than 90°.

Possible variations

For beginners:

- Take big steps but not such deep ones.

For advanced:

- The addition of hand weights.

Proportion of main motor forms of demand on physical load			
	low	medium	high
gen. endurance:	x		
strength endurance:		x	
maximal strength:		x	
speed:	x		
flexibility:			x
co-ordination:		x	

Hint

March through the whole room – it's brilliant fun!

!

29 Lunge Steps

M. quadriceps, M Glutaeus maximus
Bend and stretch with the legs wide apart!

Apparatus
A light to medium long dumb-bell or two small dumb-bells.

Description of exercise
Starting position: wide stride position
The heel of the leg behind is raised from the floor for the entire exercise i.e. only the balls of the feet are on the floor. For further weight a long dumb-bell is held on the shoulders or two small dumb-bells in the hands.

Procedure:
The legs are bent to a maximum of 90° and stretched again. The upper body is thus lowered, staying upright all the time. It's important to ensure that the feet are parallel to each other and the knees are bent facing the tips of one's toes.

Possible errors
- The weight is shifted forward.
- The back is bent.
- The knees drift inwards.
- Problems with balance.
- When straightening up again the legs are fully stretched.

Correction of errors

- Keep the heels up. Keep the upper body more upright.
- Ensure an upright posture.
- The knees and the tips of the toes are pointing in the one direction.
- Use a lighter weight. Lower the body's centre of gravity by using small extra weights which are held downwards.

Possible variations

For beginners:
- Don't use any extra weights.

For advanced:
- Use heavier weights.
- From a closed position take large steps forward and backward.

Proportion of main motor forms of demand on physical load			
	low	medium	high
gen. endurance:		X	
strength endurance:			X
maximal strength:		X	
speed:	X		
flexibility:		X	
co-ordination:		X	

Hint

This is a very hard exercise even without the use of extra weights.

!

30 Crouch (ski squats)

M. quadriceps, M. glutaeus maximus
No lower than 90°

Apparatus
- None!

Description of exercise
Starting position: stand with the legs bent
The main feature of this stance is the upper body leaning forward and an angle of approx. 90° at the knees. For aerodynamics the arms are pulled in close to the body. The centre of gravity is shifted back as far as possible.

Procedure:
Light springing movements in the knees, as in a straight downhill run on skis (a "Schuss").

Possible errors
- The knees are pushed forwards.
- Very rounded back.
- A lot of movement in the upper body.

Correction of errors

- Transfer the body weight behind.
- Tense the back muscles even more.
- The movement is concentrated in the legs.

Possible variations

For beginners:

- Light squats, not too low.
- Slight forward leaning only.

For advanced:

- Introduce a few hops and jumps in between.

Proportion of main motor forms of demand on physical load			
	low	medium	high
gen. endurance:	X		
strength endurance:			X
maximal strength:		X	
speed:	X		
flexibility:	X		
co-ordination:	X		

Hint

Good preparation for the skiing holidays!

!

31 Leg Stretches

M. quadriceps
Both knees stay together

Apparatus
- A rubber band

Description of exercise
Starting position: sitting position with knees up
The right leg is raised and stabilizes the body. The thigh of the left leg is held by the hands. The thighs and the knees are held closely together in this position, the upper body leans back and the back is straight. The rubber band is held on the floor with the lower foot and placed around the ankle of the upper leg.

Procedure:
The thigh of the upper leg stretches and bends thus pulling the rubber band apart. The knees and thighs maintain their position.

Possible errors
- The back becomes rounded.
- The rubber band gets too loose.
- The leg is pulled up towards the body.
- The entire leg is raised.

Correction of errors

- A more intensive tensing of the arms causes a more upright back position.
- The tension on the rubber band must remain.
- The knees stay together.
- Only the lower legs are to be moved up and down.

Possible variations

For beginners:

- The exercise is carried out without a rubber band.

For advanced:

- The hands are placed on the floor behind you.

Proportion of main motor forms of demand on physical load			
	low	medium	high
gen. endurance:	x		
strength endurance:		x	
maximal strength:			x
speed:	x		
flexibility:		x	
co-ordination:			x

Hint

An exercise to get used to!

83

32 Calf Lifts

M. gastrocnemius
No hopping

Apparatus
■ A step/box top
■ Wall/ ballet pole

Description of exercise
Starting position: upright standing position on the step
Only the balls of the feet on the edge of the step. The heels are lowered. Holding onto the wall or similar prevents loss of balance.

Procedure:
The feet are stretched and flexed using the ankle joint, the whole body moving up and down in the process.

Possible errors
■ Quick, springy movements.
■ There is not much strength being used in the exercise.
■ The heels are not brought down enough.

Correction of errors

■ Stress the importance of slow, accurate movement.
■ Stretch and bend the ankle slowly.
■ Make use of the entire movement radius.

Possible variations

For beginners:

■ Practise slowly.

For advanced:

■ Practise with one leg.

Proportion of main motor forms of demand on physical load			
	low	medium	high
gen. endurance:	x		
strength endurance:		x	
maximal strength:			x
speed:	x		
flexibility:		x	
co-ordination:	x		

Hint
You'll get fine sturdy calves fom this!

!

33 Supermarch

Mm. abductorens
Knees facing slightly outward, come down gently

Apparatus
■ A rubber band (wide)

Description of exercise
Starting position: upright standing position with legs lightly straddled
The rubber band is placed around the ankles. Both the feet and the knees are pointed slightly outward.

Procedure:
March on the spot. There is tension on the rubber band at all times.

Possible errors
■ The knees start turning inwards.
■ The rubber band is not tight enough.
■ The upper body moves too much.

Correction of errors

- The knees should be pointing to the toes.
- The feet to be so far apart that the rubber band can't be loose.
- Tense the trunk muscles more.

Possible variations

For beginners:

- Use a light, narrow rubber band.
- Position the rubber band above the knees.

For advanced:

- Use two rubber bands.
- Have two dumb-bells in the hands.

Proportion of main motor forms of demand on physical load			
	low	medium	high
gen. endurance:			x
strength endurance:			x
maximal strength:		x	
speed:		x	
flexibility:	x		
co-ordination:		x	

Hint

Keep on moving!

!

M. glutaeus maximus
Keep the trunk steady, don't let the head sink into the neck

Apparatus
- A mat
- A rubber band (wide or narrow)

Description of exercise
Starting position: quadruped stand with lower arms on the floor
The rubber band is placed around the ankles. The right leg is stretched out behind, keeping the band slightly taut.

Procedure:
Raise and lower the outstretched leg, thus working against the resistance of the rubber band. The back is in a fixed position so that only the posterior muscles are responsible for the movement.

Possible errors
- Hollow back position.
- Quick, sweeping movements.
- The leg on the floor begins to turn sideways.
- Upturning of the pelvis.
- The head is lifted up too high.

Correction of errors

- A strong tensing of the stomach muscles prevents the back from giving in.
- Stress the importance of slow, accurate movements.
- The toes to be pointing downwards throughout the exercise.
- Eyes are directed to the floor.

Possible variations

For beginners:

- Do without the rubber band.

For advanced:

- Use a stronger rubber band.
- Stretch out the opposite arm, then raise and lower it.

Proportion of main motor forms of demand on physical load			
	low	medium	high
gen. endurance:	x		
strength endurance:		x	
maximal strength:			x
speed:	x		
flexibility:	x		
co-ordination:			x

Hint

One can also have the lower arms leaning on a step!

35 Ischio

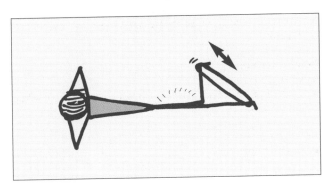

Mm. ischiocrurale
Knees together, keep the stomach tensed

Apparatus
- A rubber band
- A mat

Description of exercise
Starting position: prone position
The rubber band is placed around the ankles. The abdominal and posterior muscles are tensed the whole time to stabilize the spinal column. The thighs are on the floor, close together. The right lower leg is bent.

Procedure:
The lower leg is bent and stretched at the knee. Both the upper body and the thighs are fixed on the floor.

Possible errors
- The knees drift apart.
- Slight hollow back.
- Quick sweeping movements.
- There is not enough tension on the rubber band.

Correction of errors

- The posterior and leg muscles should be tensed to such an extent that the knees stay together.
- Tense the abdominal muscles more.
- Slower more accurate movements.
- The leg is not to be lowered to the point where the band loses its tautness.

Possible variations

For beginners:

- Do the exercise either without the rubber band entirely or with a narrow band.

For advanced:

- Use a stronger band.

Proportion of main motor forms of demand on physical load			
	low	medium	high
gen. endurance:	x		
strength endurance:		x	
maximal strength:			x
speed:	x		
flexibility:		x	
co-ordination:		x	

Hint

This is a group of muscles which is often neglected!

!

36 Heel Slides

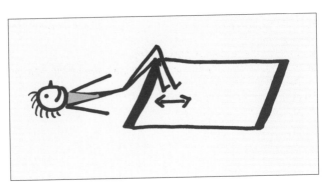

Mm. ischiocrurales
Stretch and bend the legs, bottoms up!

Apparatus
- Two carpet tiles or juggling cloths, paper towels or a slide

Description of exercise
Starting position: supine position
The feet are placed on the floor so that the heels are on the cloths or a slide. The pelvis is slightly raised, only the shoulder blades are touching the floor. The arms are lying alongside the body pressing down a little.

Procedure:
The feet slide slowly backward and forward on the slide, i.e. the legs are stretched and bent alternately. The pelvis is raised throughout the entire exercise.

Possible errors
- The back is also on the floor.
- The legs can't be brought to bend again.
- The exercise is carried out with a swinging movement.

Correction of errors

- The posterior does not touch the floor.
- Reduce the radius of movement.
- Slow, accurate movements.

Possible variations

For beginners:

- Only slightly bend and stretch the legs.
- Stretch the legs with the pelvis raised, but bend them with the back on the floor.

For advanced:

- Do the exercise with one leg.

Proportion of main motor forms of demand on physical load			
	low	medium	high
gen. endurance:	X		
strength endurance:		X	
maximal strength:			X
speed:	X		
flexibility:		X	
co-ordination:			X

Hint

It's much easier than it looks.

!

37 Leg Presses

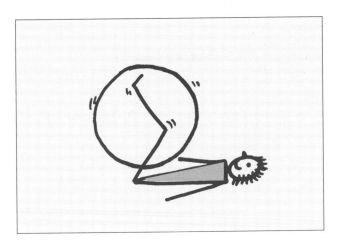

Mm. adductores
Keep the tension up at all times

Apparatus
■ A pezzi ball (max: 65 cm)

Description of exercise
Starting position: supine position
The legs are slightly bent and holding the pezzi ball in the air. To make the exercise somewhat easier, and to take the strain off the hip flexion muscles, the hands are allowed to lie under the coccyx.

Procedure:
The legs press the ball together.

Possible errors
■ The ball is dropped.
■ The legs are not upright enough.

Correction of errors
- The leg muscles are tensed at all times in order to keep hold of the ball.
- Lay hands under the coccyx.

Possible variations
For beginners:
- Use a ball which is not completely blown up.
- Use a smaller ball.

For advanced:
- Add in some crunches to train the upright stomach muscles.

Proportion of main motor forms of demand on physical load			
	low	medium	high
gen. endurance:	x		
strength endurance:		x	
maximal strength:			x
speed:	x		
flexibility:			x
co-ordination:		x	

Hint
Squashing good fun!

!

38 Rope Skipping

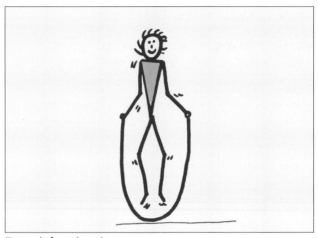

Turn only from the wrists

Apparatus
■ Speed ropes of different lengths

Description of exercise
Starting position: upright standing position
The elbows at waist level. The hands grip the handles of the skipping rope.

Procedure:
Forward turn of the rope using little momentum from the hands and wrists. Single skipping (i.e. without a skip in between) on both legs simultaneously.

Possible errors
■ Double skips when the rope is swung too fast.
■ The rope is swung using too much arm movement from the shoulder joint.
■ The landing is not soft – coming down too hard.

Correction of errors

■ Replace skips with running steps to start.
■ Refer to the turning of the wrists.
■ Land softly and don't jump so high.

Possible variations

For beginners:
■ Use slower ropes.

For advanced:
■ Try out different skips and tricks.

Proportion of main motor forms of demand on physical load			
	low	medium	high
gen. endurance:			x
strength endurance:		x	
maximal strength:	x		
speed:			x
flexibility:		x	
co-ordination:			x

Hint
Very exerting for beginners!

!

39 Knee Lifts

The entire foot is on the step

Apparatus
- A step/bench/box top

Description of exercise
Starting position: upright standing position behind the step

Procedure:
Place the right foot on the step, lift the left knee, set the left leg down on the floor, set the right leg down on the floor. Repeat, beginning with the left leg.

Possible errors
- The foot is only half on the step.
- The upper body leans back.
- The knee is lifted up too high.

Correction of errors
- Place the entire sole of the foot on the step.
- The body weight is taken by the leg which is on the step.
- The thighs should come up no higher than the horizontal.

Possible variations
For beginners:
- Select a lower step.

For advanced:
- Raise the step.
- Introduce arm movements.
- Include little jumps on the step.

Proportion of main motor forms of demand on physical load			
	low	medium	high
gen. endurance:			x
strength endurance:	x		
maximal strength:	x		
speed:		x	
flexibility:		x	
co-ordination:			x

Hint
No problem for steppers!

40 Over the Top

One, two, three, tip

Apparatus
- A step/box top

Description of exercise
Starting position: upright standing position beside the step

Procedure:
Place the right foot on the step, the left foot follows, set the right foot down on the other side of the step, left foot follows without setting down fully i. e. only tipping. Repeat to the other side.

Possible errors
- Tiptoe position.
- The tips on the floor are too firm.
- The upper body also moves in the direction of movement .

Correction of errors
- The heels must touch down on the step or floor.
- The upper body stays at the side.

Possible variations
For beginners:
- Select a lower step.

For advanced:
- Use a higher step.
- Bring in arm movements.
- Use hand weights.
- Carry out little jumps on the step.

Proportion of main motor forms of demand on physical load			
	low	medium	high
gen. endurance:			x
strength endurance:	x		
maximal strength:	x		
speed:	x		
flexibility:	x		
co-ordination:		x	

Hint
Easy to learn, also for non-steppers!

!

41 Step Hops

Swing with the step!

Apparatus
■ A medium step or a box top

Description of exercise
Starting position: upright standing position
The step is lengthways.The right foot is on the step, the left is on the floor.

Procedure:
Change sides with a little hop. Now the left foot is on the step and the right on the floor. The landing after the hop is soft, coming from the knees.

Possible errors
■ The legs are stretched.
■ The tempo is too high.
■ The participants stumble or trip.

Correction of errors
■ Go down more in the knees.
■ Little breaks are allowed.
■ Slower tempo. Lower the step.

Possible variations
For beginners:
■ The exercise can be done without the hop. The starting position is on the step. The feet tip on the floor in alternation.

For advanced:
■ Raise the step.
■ Add in arm movements to suit.
■ Quicker hops.

Proportion of main motor forms of demand on physical load			
	low	medium	high
gen. endurance:			x
strength endurance:		x	
maximal strength:	x		
speed:			x
flexibility:	x		
co-ordination:			x

Hint
Skiing is nothing compared to this.

!

Feet and knees face slightly outwards, the heels are first on the step

Apparatus
- A step/box top

Description of exercise
Starting position: upright standing position behind the step

Procedure:
The right foot is placed upon the far right hand side of the step, the left follows on the far left. The right foot steps down again behind the step, the left foot just tips down. Then repeat, this time starting with left.

Possible errors
- The foot instep is first on the step.
- The knees fall inwards.
- The upper body leans back.
- The pelvis twists with the movement.

Correction of errors

- A heel-to-toe movement is to be made.
- As in numerous other exercises, the knees point towards the toes.
- The upper body may be tilted forward a little.
- The upper body and the pelvis stay parallel to the front at all times.

Possible variations

For beginners:
- Select a lower step.

For advanced:
- Use a higher step.
- Bring in arm movements.
- Use hand weights.

Proportion of main motor forms of demand on physical load			
	low	medium	high
gen. endurance:			X
strength endurance:		X	
maximal strength:	X		
speed:	X		
flexibility:	X		
co-ordination:		X	

Hint

V-Step is easier than Basic Step!

!

43 Rebound Sprint

Fast feet

Apparatus
- A rebound/mini-trampoline

Description of exercise
Starting position: upright standing position on the rebounder

Procedure:
Sprint or running movements on the trampoline, pulling the knees up in front slightly (skips). The arms work in rhythm with the movement.

Possible errors
- Incorrect bouncing i.e. bad timing.
- The upper body leans back.

Correction of errors
- Work with and follow the trampoline movements.
- Tilting the upper body slightly forwards enables more effective training.

Possible variations

For beginners:
- Relaxed running or jumping movements.
- Marching on a rebounder.

For advanced:
- Higher knee bends.
- The use of small hand weights.

Proportion of main motor forms of demand on physical load			
	low	medium	high
gen. endurance:			X
strength endurance:		X	
maximal strength:	X		
speed:			X
flexibility:		X	
co-ordination:			X

Hint
Also possible without a trampoline (phew)!

44 Fitball Bouncing

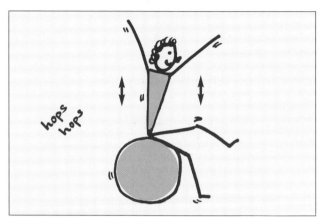

Always keep in contact with the ball

Apparatus
■ A pezzi ball (65 cm)

Description of exercise
Starting position: sitting position on the ball
The feet firmly on the floor. The ball is the correct size when the thighs are pointing slightly downwards.

Procedure:
Bobbing up and down on the ball. The legs are doing on the spot walking movements. The back remains in an upright position all the time. The arms either support the walking movement or hold the ball steady. The bottom is touching the ball at all times.

Possible errors
■ Contact with the ball is lost.
■ The upper body leans back.
■ Both feet are in the air at the same time.
■ The back loses its upright position and becomes rounded.

Correction of errors

- Don't bounce up so high that you lose the ball.
- The centre of gravity must always be over the ball.
- At least one foot must be touching the floor at a given moment.
- Tensing the abdominal and back muscles takes the strain off the spine.

Possible variations

For beginners:

- Light bouncing, but the feet stay on the floor.

For advanced:

- The feet do "jumping jack" movements.
- Bring in arm movements.

Proportion of main motor forms of demand on physical load			
	low	medium	high
gen. endurance:			X
strength endurance:		X	
maximal strength:	X		
speed:		X	
flexibility:			X
co-ordination:			X

Hint

The "aerobic version" of a spinal exercise!

!

Roll the feet well

Apparatus
- None!

Description of exercise
Procedure:
Loose, relaxed running around the circuit.

Possible errors
- Running too quickly.

Correction of errors
- Run only as fast as is aerobically possible.

Possible variations
For beginners:
- Walking

For advanced:
- A few sprints here and there.

Proportion of main motor forms of demand on physical load			
	low	medium	high
gen. endurance:			x
strength endurance:	x		
maximal strength:	x		
speed:		x	
flexibility:	x		
co-ordination:	x		

Hint

Joggers get their money's worth here!

!

46 Walking

Accurate footwork, good use of the arms

Apparatus
■ None!

Description of exercise
Procedure:
Walking quickly around the circuit. The emphasis of the walking movement lies in the deliberate rolling of the feet and the slightly exaggerated use of the arms.

Possible errors
■ Walking too slowly.
■ The feet are not rolled.
■ No use of arms.

Correction of errors
■ Walk as if one were in a hurry.
■ The rolling of the feet may also be over-exaggerated.
■ Moving the arms supports the whole walking procedure.

Possible variations

For beginners:
- Walking without using the arms.

For advanced:
- The addition of weights.

Proportion of main motor forms of demand on physical load			
	low	medium	high
gen. endurance:			x
strength endurance:	x		
maximal strength:	x		
speed:		x	
flexibility:	x		
co-ordination:		x	

Hint
For all those who never liked jogging anyway!

!

47 Cross-country Sliding

Take a big step, making good use of the arms

Apparatus
- Two carpet tiles, juggling cloths, paper towels or a slide.

Description of exercise
Starting position: stride position
The feet are on slippy cloths or a slide.

Procedure:
The legs move forward and back, just like in cross-country skiing. The movement is supported through good use of the arms. Both feet are touching the floor for the movement itself. Then the heel of the leg behind can be raised.

Possible errors
- The movement is helped along with little hops.
- The legs are only moved back while the upper body leans slightly forward.

Correction of errors

- The upper body remains in one position. Use the legs more.
- The body weight stays in the middle. Swing the legs more in the forward direction.
- Use more slippery bases.

Possible variations

For beginners:

- Hold onto the wall.

For advanced:

- Hold small weights in the hands.

Proportion of main motor forms of demand on physical load			
	low	medium	high
gen. endurance:			x
strength endurance:		x	
maximal strength:	x		
speed:		x	
flexibility:		x	
co-ordination:		x	

Hint

The best preparation for a cross-country holiday in Norway!

Strong kicks, firm punches!

Apparatus
- A step

Description of exercise
Starting position: upright standing position behind the step

Procedure:
Take a right step onto the step, a kick in the air with left, with the left foot set down again on the floor, and then with the right. The sequence is repeated again with the other leg. While kicking, punch out with the fist (right foot kick, left arm box). The kick must not be too high as the back is to remain straight.

Possible errors
- The thighs are thrown forward without any tensing of the mucles.
- The hands are not tensed.
- The back is bent for the kick.

Correction of errors
- Tensing of the legs protects the joints.
- Make firm fists.
- Kick lower. Bring more stability into the upper body.

Possible variations
For beginners:
- Leave out the arm movements.
- Lower the step.

For advanced:
- Use a high step.
- Work more with speed strength for the kick and punch.

Proportion of main motor forms of demand on physical load			
	low	medium	high
gen. endurance:			x
strength endurance:	x		
maximal strength:	x		
speed:		x	
flexibility:	x		
co-ordination:		x	

Hint
Imagine you're in a boxing ring!

!

49 Mat Boxing

Box with a strong punch against the mat!

Apparatus
- A thick jumping mat or a sand sack
- Boxing gloves

Description of exercise
Starting position: upright position before an upright jumping mat.

Procedure:
Box with alternate fists against the mat. Straight punches are particularly suitable. Tensed arms and fists are very important. The upper body supports the arm movement. The legs on the other hand are relaxed and can 'dance around'. The use of boxing gloves is recommended.

Possible errors
- The participants are standing too stiffly in front of the mat.
- The participants are afraid to punch hard.

Correction of errors

■ More leg work.
■ Begin carefully and gradually work up.

Possible variations

For beginners:
■ Take more breaks between punching.

For advanced:
■ As well as just punches, kicks against the mat can also be introduced.

Proportion of main motor forms of demand on physical load			
	low	medium	high
gen. endurance:			X
strength endurance:			X
maximal strength:		X	
speed:			X
flexibility:	X		
co-ordination:		X	

Hint
That gets aggression out of your system!

!

And volley... And dig...

Apparatus
■ A water ball or a soft ball

Description of exercise
Procedure:
Two partners pass the ball to each other by volleying and digging, or by throwing and catching it.

Possible variations
For beginners:
■ Balloons don't move as quickly.

For advanced:
■ A proper volleyball offers the well-trained group a real challenge.

Proportion of main motor forms of demand on physical load			
	low	medium	high
gen. endurance:		x	
strength endurance:	x		
maximal strength:	x		
speed:			x
flexibility:		x	
co-ordination:			x

Hint
High in fun, low in stress!

!

51 Frisbee

Rotation

Apparatus
■ A frisbee, preferably made of foam.

Description of exercise
Procedure:
Two participants pass the frisbee to each other.

Possible variations
For beginners:
■ A shorter distance between the players.

For advanced:
■ Aiming the frisbee at a goal.

Proportion of main motor forms of demand on physical load			
	low	medium	high
gen. endurance:		x	
strength endurance:	x		
maximal strength:	x		
speed:		x	
flexibility:		x	
co-ordination:			x

Hint
A foam frisbee keeps mirrors and windows intact!

!

Tock, tock

Apparatus
- A beachball game (two wooden bats, a squash ball or similar)

Description of exercise
Procedure:
Two participants hit the ball to each other.

Possible variations
For beginners:
- A middle-sized soft ball flies more predictably.

For advanced:
- Use of a tennis ball.

Proportion of main motor forms of demand on physical load			
	low	medium	high
gen. endurance:		X	
strength endurance:	X		
maximal strength:	X		
speed:			X
flexibility:		X	
co-ordination:			X

Hint

Summer sun, sand and beachball!

!

53 Bean Bag Balancing

Always keep the head up straight

Apparatus
- A thick mat/a rebounder, a bean bag

Description of exercise
Procedure:
Marching on the thick mat or rebounder. The knees should be pulled up and the bean bag balanced on the head.

Possible errors
- The ability to balance and agility are somewhat under-developed.

Correction of errors
- Slower, more accurate and controlled performance of the exercise.

Possible variations
For beginners:
- Balancing a bean bag while marching on the floor.

For advanced:
- Running on the mat.

Proportion of main motor forms of demand on physical load			
	low	medium	high
gen. endurance:		x	
strength endurance:	x		
maximal strength:	x		
speed:		x	
flexibility:		x	
co-ordination:			x

Hint
Looks hilarious but it's not as easy as you'd think!

!

Keep your eye on all the balls

Apparatus
■ Two tennis balls/two bean bags

Description of exercise
Starting position: upright standing position
A ball is held in each hand.

Procedure:
The balls are thrown up one after the other and caught again with the same hand.

Possible errors
■ The balls are passed from one hand into the other.

Correction of errors
■ The balls may only be thrown.

Possible variatios

For beginners:
- One ball is thrown from one hand to the other.
- One ball is thrown up and caught with the one hand.

For advanced:
- Two balls are held in one hand, thrown up after each other and caught again in the same hand.
- Juggling with three balls.

Proportion of main motor forms of demand on physical load			
	low	medium	high
gen. endurance:	x		
strength endurance:	x		
maximal strength:	x		
speed:			x
flexibility:		x	
co-ordination:			x

Hint

When you've understood the principle of it all, it's not half as difficult!

!

55 Whoops!

Think first, then throw

Apparatus
- A juggling cloth
- A tennis ball

Description of exercise
Starting position: upright standing position
Hold a tennis ball in one hand, in the other hand a juggling cloth.

Procedure:
Bounce the tennis ball onto the floor and throw the cloth up in the air, either simultaneously or one after the other. Catch them again before they hit the floor or come back down.

Possible errors
- The time gap between throwing and bouncing is too wide.
- Problems of co-ordination.

Correction of errors
- Refer to the importance of simultaneous actions.
- Take time doing the movement i. e. don't rush it.

Possible variations
For beginners:
- Throw up the cloth and catch it and then bounce the ball and catch it.

For advanced:
- Swap hands.

Proportion of main motor forms of demand on physical load			
	low	medium	high
gen. endurance:	x		
strength endurance:	x		
maximal strength:	x		
speed:			x
flexibility:	x		
co-ordination:			x

Hint
When you've got the hang of it, it's a successful exercise!

!

56 Balloon Fight

Keep everything under control

Apparatus
■ Four balloons for two people.

Description of exercise
Starting position: upright standing position
A balloon is held between the knees or the ankles.

Procedure:
Two participants pass the balloons to each other simultaneously.

Possible errors
■ Movements are too hectic.

Correction of errors
■ Pass the ballons higher.

Possible variations

For beginners:

- Cut down on the amount of balloons.
- No passing to the other person, each person tries to keep their own balloon under control.

For advanced:

- Three balloons per person.
- Five balloons for two people.

Proportion of main motor forms of demand on physical load			
	low	medium	high
gen. endurance:		x	
strength endurance:	x		
maximal strength:	x		
speed:		x	
flexibility:	x		
co-ordination:			x

Hint
Keep calm!

!

5 Sample Lessons

The following training lessons provide a guideline when planning a session of circuit training. Different target groups, and possible variations according to training load, are taken into consideration here. Certain important factors are mentioned beforehand.

Within every circuit exercises in supine or prone position should not be a follow-up station to intensive exercises for the cardiovascular system. As well as feeling unwell the blood pressure would also shoot up too quickly by this. Therefore, instead of having an endurance station before exercises in supine or prone position, a power station, for example for arm and leg muscles, is recommended e.g. first press ups, then stomach exercises.

The sample lessons are set in such a way that two people can train at each station. This has proved to be of great advantage if the appropriate number of stations can be set up; the participants are better motivated through more variety and the "company". It's simply better training in twos.

It goes without saying that the trainer must not be a training participant at the stations, but someone who walks around, corrects and motivates where necessary, takes a look at the clock now and then; basically, he has everything under control in the lesson.

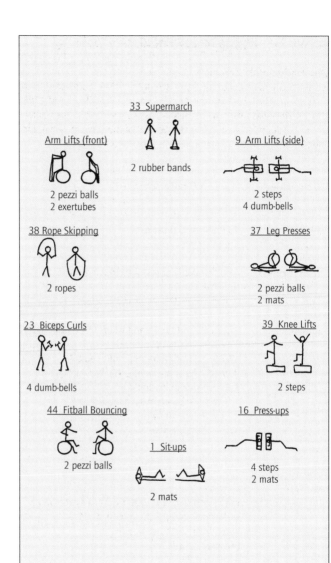

33 Supermarch

Arm Lifts (front)

2 pezzi balls
2 exertubes

2 rubber bands

9 Arm Lifts (side)

2 steps
4 dumb-bells

38 Rope Skipping

2 ropes

37 Leg Presses

2 pezzi balls
2 mats

23 Biceps Curls

4 dumb-bells

39 Knee Lifts

2 steps

44 Fitball Bouncing

2 pezzi balls

1 Sit-ups

2 mats

16 Press-ups

4 steps
2 mats

Description and Comments

Within this circuit endurance and strength stations alternate with each other. The resulting alternating demands on legs and arms proves to be pleasant as well as helpful, as it prevents total exhaustion of the muscles affected in each case. Several of the exercises are not in original form, if so the variation form is then used.

Target group: averagely trained people

Intervals: 60 sec load/20 sec rest

Organisation: up to 20 participants can train in twos at the stations.

Sequence

5 min	setting up and words of explanation
10 min	warm up
13 min	station training (one round)
5 min	group training (aerobics step combinations)
13 min	station training (one round)
4 min	cool down
10 min	stretching

Total apparatus required:

six mats
eight steps/two box tops and four small boxes
eight dumb-bells: four light, four heavy
two rubber bands (difficult)
two exertubes (easy)
six pezzi balls
two skipping ropes

23 Bizeps Curls

4 dumb bells

5 Sit-ups

1 high step
2 mats

37 Leg Presses

2 pezzi balls
2 mats

42 V-Step

2 steps

17 Flying

4 dumb bells

56 Balloon Fight

3 balloons

32 Calf Lifts

2 steps

46 Walking

around the circuit

21 Back Lifts

2 sticks

Leg Lifts

2 -steps

53 Bean Bag Balancing

1 thick mat
bean bags

40 Over the Top

2 -steps

5.2 Circuit Training for Beginners

Description and Comments
For this circuit exercises are selected which are easy to grasp by beginners. The movement is low to medium-strong load in order to prevent over-taxing. Play and co-ordination exercises takes the "hard training" away.

Target group:	Beginners with little or no experience of sport and in poor training condition
Intervals:	45 sec load/20 sec rest
Organisation:	Up to 24 participants can train in twos at twelve stations.

Sequence:

5 min	setting up and words of explanation
10 min	warm up
13 min	station training (one round)
5 min	group training (loosening exercises)
13 min	station training (one round)
4 min	cool down
10 min	stretching

Total apparatus required:

four mats
nine steps/five box tops and three small boxes
eight dumb-bells
two pezzi balls
three balloons
two sticks
a thick mat/two rebounders
two bean bags

28 Mud Walking

up and down the circuit

19 Weight Lifting

1 high step
2 exertubes

24 Dips

3 steps

26 Squats

2 steps

4 Hip Lifts

2 mats

45 Jogging

around the circuit

38 Rope Skipping

2 ropes

30 Crouch /Ski Squats

16 Press-ups

2 steps
2 mats

5.3 Advanced Circuit Training

Description and Comments
In the set-up and selection of exercises, movements are chosen here
which are either challenging for co-ordination or physically very
demanding. The participants must be familiar with most of the
exercises and how they are to be performed.

Target group:	participants who are well-trained or experienced in circuit training
Intervals:	60 sec load/15 sec rest
Organisation:	18 participants train in twos at each station.

Sequence:	5 min	setting up and words of explanation
	10 min	warm up
	23 min	station training (2 rounds)
	12 min	group strength training (e.g. abdominal muscle exercises)
	10 min	stretching

**Total apparatus
required:**   four mats
eight steps/four box tops and four small boxes
two exertubes (easy)
two skipping ropes

19 Weight Lifting

1 high step
2 exertubes

31 Leg Stretches

2 mats
2 rubber bands

24 Dips

3 steps

18 Arm Lifts (front)

4 dumb bells

35 Ischio

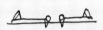

2 mats
2 rubber bands

12 Rubber Band Pulling

2 rubber bands

16 Press-ups

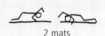

2 mats

4 Hip Lifts

9 Arm Side Lifts

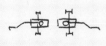

2 mats

2 steps
4 dumb bells

5.4 Maximal Strength Circuit

Description and Comments

The exercises chosen here can, through performance or the addition of further pieces of apparatus, be varied in load to become maximal strength training. The right degree of demand has been selected when it is just barely possible to carry out the exercises within the load interval. This would be approximately 8-14 repetitions depending on the tempo of music and range of movement.

Target group:	Advanced participants who are familiar with the performance of the exercises.
Intervals:	30 sec load/30 sec rest
Organisation:	18 participants can do three rounds of station training in twos.

Sequence:

5 min	setting up and words of explanation
15 min	warm-up
27 min	station training (three rounds)
3 min	cool down
10 min	stretching

Total apparatus required:

eight mats
six steps/three box tops, one inlay, three small boxes
eight dumb-bells: approx: 4x5 kg and 4x2 kg
six rubber bands (difficult)
two exertubes (difficult)

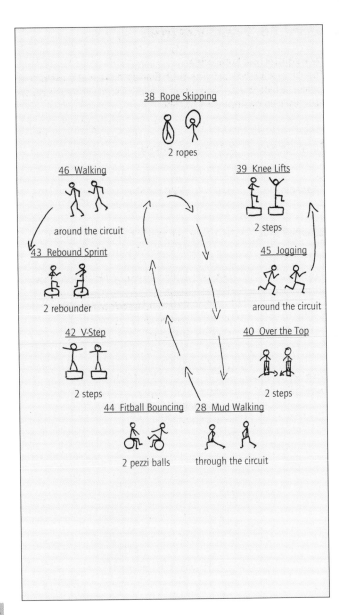

38 Rope Skipping

2 ropes

46 Walking

around the circuit

39 Knee Lifts

2 steps

43 Rebound Sprint

2 rebounder

45 Jogging

around the circuit

42 V-Step

2 steps

40 Over the Top

2 steps

44 Fitball Bouncing

2 pezzi balls

28 Mud Walking

through the circuit

5.5 Endurance Circuit

Description and Comments

The concept of this circuit is such that each station is relevant to general endurance or strength endurance. The main emphasis here lies clearly on cardiovascular training.

Target group: the averagely trained

Intervals: 90 sec load/20 sec rest

Organisation: 18 people can train in twos at each station

Sequence:
5 min	setting up and words of explanation
10 min	warm up
33 min	station training (two rounds)
4 min	cool down
10 min	stretching

Total apparatus required:
six steps
two rebounders
two pezzi balls
two ropes

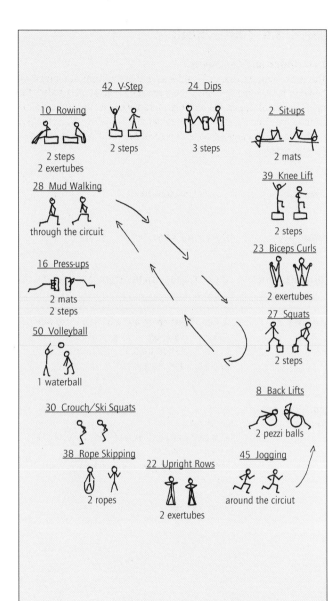

42 V-Step

24 Dips

10 Rowing

2 steps

3 steps

2 steps
2 exertubes

2 Sit-ups

2 mats

28 Mud Walking

through the circuit

39 Knee Lift

2 steps

16 Press-ups

2 mats
2 steps

23 Biceps Curls

2 exertubes

50 Volleyball

1 waterball

27 Squats

2 steps

30 Crouch/Ski Squats

8 Back Lifts

2 pezzi balls

38 Rope Skipping

2 ropes

22 Upright Rows

2 exertubes

45 Jogging

around the circiut

5.6 Power Circuit

Description and Comments

This is a colourfully mixed circuit for several participants. It's important however to note the following: the more stations that are needed, the more pieces of apparatus and the more variety in the exercises are needed too. This means that the trainer must organise the setting-up of the stations well in advance to prevent too much time being spent for this phase.

Target group: the averagely trained

Intervals: 60 sec load/15 sec rest

Organisation: Up to 30 people can train in twos at each station.

Sequence:

5 min	setting up and words of explanation.
9 min	warm up
38 min	station training (two rounds)
8 min	stretching

Total apparatus required:

four mats
13 steps/four benches and four box tops and three small boxes.
six exertubes: four easy and two difficult ones
two ropes
a waterball
two pezzi balls

5 Sit-ups

2 mats
1 high step

24 Dips

2 steps

40 Over the Top

1 step

51 Frisbee

1 frisbee

52 Beachball

1 beachball game

39 Knee Lifts

1 step

13 Do It Together

2 rubber bands

16 Press-ups

2 mats
2 steps

27 Squats

2 rubber bands

5.7 Partner Circuit

Description and Comments

The majority of the exercises in this circuit can only be carried out with a partner, direct body contact is avoided however. When there is an odd number of participants the trainer must often stand in for the missing partner.

Target group: averagely trained participants, who know each other to some extent.

Intervals: 60 sec load/20 sec rest

Organisation: Up to 18 people can train in twos at any station.

Sequence:

5 min	setting up and words of explanation
10 min	warm up
12 min	station training (one round)
5 min	group endurance training (e.g. walking)
12 min	station training (one round)
6 min	cool down
10 min	stretching

Total apparatus required:

seven steps
four rubber bands
a frisbee
a beachball game

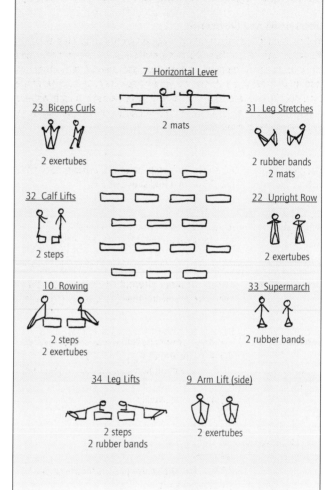

7 Horizontal Lever
2 mats

23 Biceps Curls
2 exertubes

31 Leg Stretches
2 rubber bands
2 mats

32 Calf Lifts
2 steps

22 Upright Row
2 exertubes

10 Rowing
2 steps
2 exertubes

33 Supermarch
2 rubber bands

34 Leg Lifts
2 steps
2 rubber bands

9 Arm Lift (side)
2 exertubes

5.8 Circuit Training and Step-Aerobics

Description and Comments
In this form of circuit training station training and step-aerobics
alternate with each other. The participants train at the stations, then
move on to group training on the steps, and then go on to the next
station. The step intervals may be longer than the load intervals at the
stations. Due to the high demand on the cardiovascular systems
during the step intervals exercises in prone or supine position are to be
avoided at the stations.

Target group: Averagely trained people with experience of both
circuit training and step aerobics.

Intervals: 60 sec load at a station/15 sec rest
120 sec load on the steps/15 sec rest

Organisation: 18 participants alternate between training in
twos at a station and then in a group on the steps.

Sequence:

5 min	setting up and words of explanation.
10 min	warm up
30 min	station and step training (one round)
5 min	cool down
10 min	stretching

**Total apparatus
required:**   two mats
18 steps for the centre plus six for the circuit
six rubber bands
eight exertubes

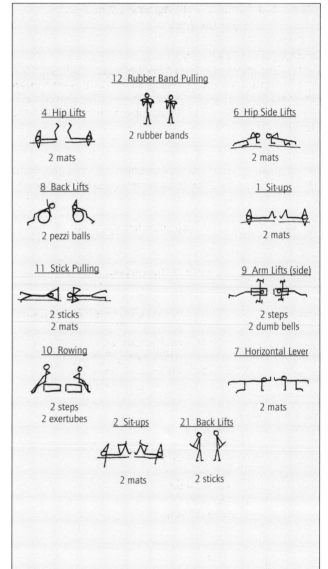

12 Rubber Band Pulling
2 rubber bands

4 Hip Lifts
2 mats

6 Hip Side Lifts
2 mats

8 Back Lifts
2 pezzi balls

1 Sit-ups
2 mats

11 Stick Pulling
2 sticks
2 mats

9 Arm Lifts (side)
2 steps
2 dumb bells

10 Rowing
2 steps
2 exertubes

7 Horizontal Lever
2 mats

2 Sit-ups
2 mats

21 Back Lifts
2 sticks

5.9 Circuit Training as Part of Spine Gymnastics

Description and Comments

The following lesson can not only be used as a special highlight within spine gymnastics but can also be integrated into circuit training as an intensive training session for the trunk muscles. The prerequisite in both cases is, however, that the participants are familiar with the exercises.

Target group: more advanced participants of spine gymnastics, or averagely trained participants of circuit training.

Intervals: 60 sec load/20 sec rest

Organisation: 22 people can train in twos.

Sequence:
5 min	setting up and words of explanation
10 min	warm up
3 min	mobilization exercises
29 min	station training (two rounds)
13 min	stretching and relaxation

Total apparatus required:
twelve mats
two steps
four dumb-bells
two rubber bands
two exertubes
four sticks
two pezzi balls

12 Rubber Band Pulling

2 rubber bands

39 Knee Lifts

2 steps

44 Fitball Bouncing

2 pezzi balls

23 Biceps Curls

4 dumb bells

22 Upright Rows

2 exertubes

33 Supermarch

2 rubber bands

43 Rebounding

2 rebounders

8 Back Lifts

2 sticks

40 Over the Top

2 steps

Description and Comments

This circuit is particularly suitable for the older generation as it is easy to vary the load of the individual exercises. None of the exercises involve tedious lying on the ground or standing up again. The basic positions at the different stations are relatively easy to assume. They do not raise blood pressure but they are relatively challenging however from a co-ordination point of view.

Target group: averagely trained older participants with some experience of circuit exercises.

Intervals: 1st round: 30 sec load/30 sec rest
2nd round: 45 sec load/30 sec rest

Organisation: 18 participants train in twos at each station.

Sequence:

5 min	setting up and words of explanation
15 min	warm up
9 min	station training (one round)
1 min	rest, loosening exercises
12 min	station training (one round)
6 min	cool down
12 min	stretching

Total apparatus required:

four steps
four dumb-bells
four rubber bands
two rebounders
two exertubes
two sticks
two balls

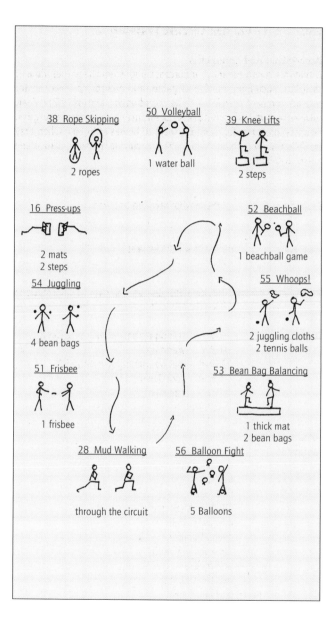

38 Rope Skipping
2 ropes

50 Volleyball
1 water ball

39 Knee Lifts
2 steps

16 Press-ups
2 mats
2 steps

54 Juggling
4 bean bags

51 Frisbee
1 frisbee

52 Beachball
1 beachball game

55 Whoops!
2 juggling cloths
2 tennis balls

53 Bean Bag Balancing
1 thick mat
2 bean bags

28 Mud Walking
through the circuit

56 Balloon Fight
5 Balloons

5.11 Playful Circuit Training

Description and Comments

Within this circuit the most important thing is not the actual training itself but much more the fun of games and movement. However not only are forms of exercise such as co-ordination and flexibility, dealt with here but also strength and endurance. Certain energetic exercises, press ups for example, seem to be easier to bear when they are followed by a "play" station. This circuit of course is particularly suited to children.

Target group: all those who have fun at games

Intervals: 60 sec load/20 sec rest

Organisation: 24 participants can train in twos at each station.

Sequence:

5 min	setting up and words of explanation
10 min	warm up
32 min	station training (two rounds)
3 min	cool down
10 min	stretching

Total aparatus required:

four mats
one thick mat
four steps
two ropes
one beachball game
one water ball
five balloons
two juggling cloths
one frisbee
two tennis balls
six bean bags

68 French Press

2 exertubes

13 Do It Together

2 rubber bands

36 Heel Slides

2 slides or 4 cloths

3 Foot Slides

2 slides or 4 cloths

44 Fitball Bouncing

2 pezzi balls

47 Cross-country Sliding

2 slides or 4 cloths

41 Step Hops

2 steps

43 Rebound Sprint

2 rebounders

24 Dips

3 steps

29 Lunge Steps

2 long dumbbells

Description and Comments

This circuit brings variety into skiing exercises. The exercises selected are suitable both for downhill or cross-country skiers. Apart from the well-known exercises for the legs, the humeral muscles, in particular the triceps, are also strengthened here. These muscles are especially important after a fall in order to be able to free oneself out of the deep snow.

Both downhill and cross-country skiing have a lot to do with stamina and endurance and for this reason a longer load phase is recommended. For certain muscle-intensive exercises e.g. dips, little breaks are allowed.

Target group:	averagely trained people, holiday skiers
Intervals:	60-90 seconds load/ 20 seconds rest
Organisation:	22 participants can train in twos at each station.

Sequence:		
	3 min	setting up and words of explanation
	10 min	warm up
	33 min	station training (2 rounds)
	4 min	cool down
	10 min	stretching

Total apparatus required:

five steps
two rebounder
two pezzi balls
two rubber bands
two exertubes
six slides or 12 cloths
two long dumb-bells

49 Mat Boxing

1 thick mat, 2 pairs
of boxing gloves

3 Foot Slides

2 slides or 4 cloths

24 Dips

3 steps

29 Lunge Steps

2 long dumbbells

38 Rope Skipping

2 ropes

16 Press-ups

2steps, 2 mats

6 Hip Side Lifts

2 mats

48 Step-Kick-Box

2 steps

20 Shoulder Press

2 steps

5.13 Kick and Box Circuit

Description and Comments

Kick boxing has become really popular recently. In the fitness area, the trend is heading towards simple but effective training which is also fun at the same time. Kick boxing is just the right thing for this target group. This circuit is a perfect supplement to normal training sessions and its structure means that even non kick-boxers can profit from it too. One does not have to be a specialist to stand tall in this circuit, but one should be relatively fit, otherwise there's some awful muscle soreness the next day!

So, it's not just about kick and box movements here, but body tension and strength are dealt with too.

Everything needed for this form of sport can be found here. There is just as much emphasis on arm strength as on trunk stabilization or on the typical kick and box movements. And you can let off steam as well.

Target Group:	well-trained, kick boxing fans
Intervals:	60 seconds load/20 seconds rest
Organisation:	18 participants can train in twos at each station.

Sequence:

3 min	setting up and words of explanation
10 min	warm-up
12 min	station training (1 round)
9 min	shadow-boxing or -kicking
12 min	station training (1 round)
4 min	cool down
10 min	stretching

Total apparatus required:

one thick mat or a punchbag
two pairs of boxing gloves
seven steps
two slides or four cloths
four long dumbbells
four mats
two ropes

6 That Took Some Doing!

Now, towards the end of this handbook I would like to wish all trainers a lot of fun and even more success with their own circuit training sessions! I hope that I have provided you with enough suggestions and ideas.

I also hope that this may be the beginning of further developments for 'training in a circle'. With basic knowledge and a certain amount of creativity, many variations are possible. There is undoubtedly a large number of other possibilities and other pieces of apparatus, all of which prevent circuit training from ever becoming boring. The main thing is that one doesn't keep going round in a circle?!

Ulli Heldt

For ...
your Fitness!

Dieter Koschel
Allround Fitness
The Beginner's Guide

"Allround Fitness" by Dieter Koschel explains his popular and proven approach to fitness, incorporating both basic training principles and the all important element of fun. Designed as a guide for fitness instructors, teachers and personal training, the book describes a well thought out, basic programme consisting of gymnastic exercises, cardio vascular training and relaxation techniques. It provides the fitness professional with many practical tips for organising a course including time planning, publicity, financial aspects.

120 pages, 37 photos
10 tables and 17 figures
paperback, 14.8 x 21 cm
ISBN 1-84126-011-8
£ 9.95 UK/$ 14.95 US/
$ 20.95 CDN

Klaus Bös/Joachim Saam
Walking
Fitness & Health through Everyday Activity

This book describes the basics of walking technique, considers the necessary clothing, the appropriate medical background, and also gives advice on diet.
It provides interesting incentives for the professional as well as the beginner, like schemes for strengthening the whole body or tips for new kinds of walking e.g. body walking (meditative walking).
Keen leisure sportsmen and inveterate sporting buffs alike will find their way into the best sort of healthy training, where the emphasis is on enjoyment.

112 pages, 20 photos
paperback, 11.5 x 18 cm
ISBN 1-84126-001-0
£ 5.95 UK/$ 8.95 US/
$ 12.95 CDN

MEYER & MEYER Verlag | Von-Coels-Straße 390 | D-52080 Aachen | Fax + +49 (0)2 41/9 58 10-10